English Language Standards in Higher Education

From entry to exit

Sophie Arkoudis, Chi Baik
and **Sarah Richardson**

Foreword by **Simon Marginson**

ACER Press

First published 2012

by ACER Press, an imprint of
Australian Council for Educational Research Ltd
19 Prospect Hill Road, Camberwell
Victoria, 3124, Australia

www.acerpress.com.au
sales@acer.edu.au

Text copyright © Sophie Arkoudis, Chi Baik and Sarah Richardson 2012
Design and typography copyright © ACER Press 2012

This book is copyright. All rights reserved. Except under the conditions described in the Copyright Act 1968 of Australia and subsequent amendments, and any exceptions permitted under the current statutory licence scheme administered by Copyright Agency Limited (www.copyright.com.au), no part of this publication may be reproduced, stored in a retrieval system, transmitted, broadcast or communicated in any form or by any means, optical, digital, electronic, mechanical, photocopying, recording or otherwise, without the written permission of the publisher.

Project edited by Rebecca Leech
Edited by Sandra Goldbloom Zurbo
Indexed by Russell Brooks

Cover design, text design and typesetting by ACER Project Publishing
Cover image © lucadp, used under licence from Shutterstock.com
Printed in Australia by BPA Print Group

National Library of Australia Cataloguing-in-Publication entry:

Author: Arkoudis, Sophie.

Title:	English language standards in higher education : from entry to exit / Sophie Arkoudis, Chi Baik and Sarah Richardson.
ISBN:	9781742860640 (pbk.)
Notes:	Includes bibliographical references and index.
Subjects:	English language--Acquisition. Academic achievement. English language--Study and teaching (Higher)--Standards. English language--Study and teaching (Higher)--Foreign speakers

Other Authors/Contributors:
　　　　　　　　Baik, Chi
　　　　　　　　Richardson, Sarah.

Dewey Number:　　401.93

This book is printed on carbon neutral paper derived from well-managed forests and other controlled sources certified against Forest Stewardship Council® standards, a non-profit organisation devoted to encouraging the responsible management of the world's forests.

FOREWORD

Simon Marginson
Centre for the Study of Higher Education,
University of Melbourne

This clear and accessible book brings together two practical problems in higher education and provides them with a joint solution. It is the first work to do so and for this reason is likely to achieve an enduring importance for educators. The impact of the book will extend beyond Australia, where its examples are set, because the problems are common to higher education and international education throughout the English-speaking world and beyond.

The first problem is the English language proficiency (ELP) of students in all disciplines, particularly English as an additional language (EAL) students, students from home and school backgrounds where English is not the primary medium. This is one-third of the students in Australian higher education institutions, including 200 000 international students. The historically inherited approach to this problem, at least in relation to international students (local students with ELP issues were and are largely unrecognised) is simply to set a test barrier at the point of entry and expect students to take responsibility for their own language-related development. In this, the dominant way of thinking – or, more strictly, of not thinking – about ELP is that the degree program is designed to be developmental and cumulative, but language development, which follows a similar logic, is ignored. The implication is that the language medium and program contents are wholly separable, and institutions can use this distinction to limit their commitment to students. But in the past half decade there has been increasing recognition that this approach is not good enough. ELP is a key issue that teachers and their institutions must address, one that is integral to standards in tertiary education, and affects domestic as well as international students – more so as post-school

[Foreword

education spreads inexorably across the whole population. Concern about the ELP issue has been deepened by research showing that some international students graduate with ELP levels no better than those they achieved in testing at the beginning of their studies. As the authors state, 'ensuring that support for English language improvement is central is becoming increasingly essential.'

The second problem is that of the workplace readiness of all graduates, whether EAL or not. This has been an issue of employer and public concern for at least two decades, generating much discussion about the generic skills needed in the workplace; about the extent to which those skills are domain-specific (nested in and varying according to disciplinary knowledge and professional training), and the extent to which they are common across all programs; and about how to embed work preparation and skill development into curricula and assessment. In many institutions there has been progress in developing work experience programs, but there is as yet no consensus on the core question about skill development – solely generic or domain specific also? – and many disciplinary practitioners still ignore work-readiness, leaving it 'to the students'. This neglect tends to reinforce the neglect also of ELP among EAL students (and ELP for graduates), though we know that a primary reason why many international students enter English-speaking countries is to acquire workplace English.

It is obvious that both problems constitute unmet needs on a large scale. It is obvious that both are matters of student welfare and public interest. Yet, remarkable as it sounds, it has been proven difficult to lodge these issues in the mainstream of teaching and learning in higher education. It has been difficult to reconcile discipline-based learning and professional preparation with on one hand English language proficiency, and on the other hand work-related skills, such as communication and teamwork. In part this has been a problem of resources limitations, lack of specialist expertise and a crowded curriculum. But behind every problem of crowding or resource limitation there is a question about priorities. The plain fact is that higher education institutions have been unable to make ELP a priority. There is much variation in the extent to which and the manner in which ELP is explicitly embedded in teaching. Rather than being treated as a core learning issue, it tends to be pathologised and marginalised. It becomes sidelined into low status remedial programs provided by under-resourced specialists who are given little respect by disciplinary academics. So there is little cooperation between the specialist language teachers and subject teachers. There is even more variation in the integration of ELP in assessment, where practices are so inconsistent as to be counterproductive and unjust. Higher education institutions lack an agreed means by which to monitor and evaluate students' language skills. Frankly, many academics do not know what to do. This is where *English Language Standards in Higher Education: From entry to exit* comes in.

What is the recipe that Sophie Arkoudis, Chi Baik and Sarah Richardson bring to the table? As the authors state, the objective of the book is to ensure 'that EAL students graduate with the necessary English language skills for use in the workplace or further study'. All graduates, with no exceptions, should be operating at professional levels of English language competence in listening, speaking, reading and writing. This objective should be equally mandatory for institutions and their students and built into all curricula and assessment requirements. What constitutes language competence varies by field, while also containing generic elements common to all fields. How do we get there? The authors' chosen solution is what they call the 'developmental model' for building language competence. Like the welfare state notion of 'cradle to grave' social policy, the authors offer the idea of an educational continuum lasting for the duration of tertiary studies and beyond. There are three main phases in the continuum: entry, experience and exit. The three phases are closely related. English language testing at entry (which, they explain, should be only one means of student selection, and one way of diagnosing learning issues) is only the beginning of the process of identifying and addressing language development. ELP acquisition should not be seen as a 'foundational' strategy but an ongoing aspect of the whole degree program, culminating in the formation of the work-related communication skills that are crucial for graduates at exit and beyond.

A strength of *English Language Standards in Higher Education: From entry to exit* is its practical approach to the nuanced educational relationship between the English language, as medium of instruction and expression, and the content of learning. Paradoxically, language and discipline are separable: each requires distinctive

v

Foreword

teaching, and also integrated teaching, in that both are learned together. Language is the medium in which content is expressed, while disciplines have distinctive languages of their own, so that we have English for accounting, English for architecture and so on. In short, there is both a generic element and a domain-specific element in language use and development. To focus only on the generic element in language and communication is to weaken language learning by missing specialised language needs, marginalising that language learning (the discipline is where status resides) and creating a second, implicit and possibly contrary approach to ELP in the work of the disciplinary teacher. To focus only on the specialised element is in language and communication is to leave ELP solely in the hands of disciplinary teachers who mostly lack specialised knowledge of ELP and accordingly, are likely to leave language issues as implicit, or handle them inconsistently. Both must be addressed; and both kinds of teaching specialist have a part to play, in close cooperation with each other.

The developmental approach is summarised and explained in the opening and closing chapters. The body of the book reviews international student entry (Chapter 2), the student experience of ELP programs (Chapter 3) and integration of ELP into curricula and assessment (Chapters 4 and 5). Chapters 6 and 7 extend the developmental approach in two ways. Chapter 6 makes suggestions for improving the interaction between local and international students, where ELP is both a barrier to be overcome and a principal outcome of finding common ground between the two groups. Chapter 7 takes the argument into offshore programs in EAL settings. Chapter 8 focuses on ELP for the workplace. Chapter 9 brings all of these themes together to underline the point that English language learning is not only domain specific in terms of knowledge and occupational training, but contextually specific in terms of the cultural setting. Teaching and learning strategies need to fully embrace the context if they are to be effective. When all these elements – language and its use, knowledge domain, and cultural context – are at the same time understood specifically and combined effectively, then we will be really cooking!

CONTENTS

Foreword
Simon Marginson — iii

List of tables — viii

List of figures — ix

Acronyms — x

Acknowledgements — xii

About the authors — xiii

Chapter 1 English: The language of higher education — 1

Chapter 2 English language entry standards — 17

Chapter 3 Models of English language programs — 37

Chapter 4 Integrating English language learning in the disciplines — 61

Chapter 5 Curriculum design and assessment of English language proficiency in the disciplines — 79

Chapter 6 Designing curricula to enhance interaction — 93

Chapter 7 English language development in offshore education — 113

Chapter 8 English language proficiency and workplace readiness — 131

Chapter 9 What does it take to ensure English language standards? — 156

References — 166

Index — 182

TABLES

Table 2.1	Overview of four English tests	24
Table 2.2	Examples of Common European Frame of Reference global scales	26
Table 2.3	Comparing test scores	27
Table 3.1	Academic language and learning activities in Australian higher education institutions	40
Table 3.2	Models of collaboration	44
Table 4.1	Summary of student evaluations in English for academic purposes	70
Table 4.2	Pass rate and average mark for students in European architecture	71
Table 5.1	Features of writing academics consider very important	82
Table 5.2	Typology of academic practices in responding to students' writing	85
Table 5.3	Assessment practices to support the development of English language proficiency	91
Table 7.1	Continuities of practice in onshore and offshore curricula	128
Table 8.1	Most important skills and attributes required of recruiting graduates	133
Table 8.2	Importance of skills and personal attributes to graduate recruiters and students	140

FIGURES

Figure 1.1 English language proficiency developmental continuum 13

Figure 5.1 Curriculum designed to develop written English language proficiency in an economics course 90

Figure 6.1 The interaction for learning framework 97

Figure 7.1 Different aspects of developing offshore programs 127

ACRONYMS

AALL	Association for Academic Language and Learning
AEI	Australian Education International
AHELO	Assessment of Higher Education Learning Outcomes
ALL	academic language and learning
ALTC	Australian Learning and Teaching Council (now the Office for Learning and Teaching)
AQF	Australian Qualifications Framework
AVCC	Australian Vice-Chancellors' Committee
CAE	Certificate in Advanced English
CEFR	Common European Framework of Reference
DEEWR	Department of Education, Employment and Workplace Relations
EAL	English as an additional language
EAP	English for academic purposes
ELICOS	English Language Intensive Courses for Overseas Students
ELP	English language proficiency
ESL	English as a second language
ESOL	English for speakers of other languages
IDP Australia	an international student placement service
IEAA	International Education Association of Australia
IELTS	International English Language Testing System
MASUS	a procedure for Measuring the Academic Skills of University Students

Acronyms

OECD	Organisation for Economic Co-operation and Development
OET	Occupational English Test
OLT	Office for Learning and Teaching (a DEEWR initiative)
PELA	post-enrolment language assessment
PISA	Programme for International Student Assessment
PR	permanent residency
PTE	Pearson Test of English
SAT	Scholastic Aptitude Test
TEQSA	Tertiary Education Quality and Standards Agency
TESOL	teaching English to speakers of other languages
TOEFL	Test of English as a Foreign Language
TOEFL iBT	Test of English as a Foreign Language internet-based test
TOEFL PBT	Test of English as a Foreign Language paper-based test
VET	vocational education and training

ACKNOWLEDGEMENTS

We are grateful to the following organisations for permission to reproduce previously published material: the Centre for the Study of Higher Education at the University of Melbourne for material from *Teaching International Students* (2006), and the Department of Education, Employment and Workplace Relations for material from the report *Good Practice Principles for English Language Proficiency for International Students in Australian Universities* (2008), the report *The Impact of English Language Proficiency and Workplace Readiness on the Employment Outcomes of Tertiary International Students* (2009) and the project *Finding Common Ground: Enhancing interaction between domestic and international students* (2010).

Sophie Arkoudis and Chi Baik would like to thank Richard James and Simon Marginson from the Centre for the Study of Higher Education at the University of Melbourne for their support and encouragement during the writing of this book. Thanks also to Michelle Van Kampen for the illustrations and to Caterina Ho for her administrative support. Sarah Richardson would like to thank the higher education team at the Australian Council for Educational Research. All the authors would like to thank Debbie Lee and Rebecca Leech from ACER Press.

Finally, we thank our families: Philip, Joanna and Zoe Jellie; Binny, Amy, Jess and Katie Baik; and Rosemary and Mike Richardson, Helen, James and Emma Todd and Graham Wells.

ABOUT THE AUTHORS

Associate Professor Sophie Arkoudis is Deputy Director of the Centre for the Study of Higher Education, University of Melbourne. Her research is associated with higher education policy development. She has published widely, and is a regular keynote speaker and media commentator on English language proficiency for international students in higher education. In 2012, she received an Australian Government Office for Learning and Teaching National Senior Teaching Fellowship to work on embedding English language learning in higher education curricula.

Dr Chi Baik is a Senior Lecturer in the Centre for the Study of Higher Education, University of Melbourne. She has conducted large research projects and written widely on issues related to assessment, internationalisation of university curricula and peer learning among diverse students.

Dr Sarah Richardson is a Senior Research Fellow at the Australian Council for Educational Research. She works on national and international research projects in higher education, and has extensive experience as a teacher of English as a Second Language, an examiner for the International English Language Testing System and a university tutor and lecturer.

CHAPTER 1

ENGLISH: THE LANGUAGE OF HIGHER EDUCATION

English is currently the international language of higher education. It has become an ever more commonplace medium of instruction in higher education institutions around the world. In some cases, higher education institutions in non-English-speaking countries choose to offer part or all of their degrees in English. In other cases, students travel outside of their countries of origin to attain a higher education in an English-speaking country. Both approaches are used so students can gain the language skills that their working lives are likely to demand of them. At the same time, the movement of people around the world ensures that many countries have an increasingly multicultural population. As a consequence, it can no longer be assumed that the language that a student speaks at home corresponds with the language of instruction at their institution.

Whether Chinese students are studying accounting in New York, Iraqi immigrant students are studying biology in Sydney or Russian students are studying engineering in Moscow, a similar set of challenges is raised for the institutions in which they are enrolled. What level of English is required for students to be able to cope with the demands of tertiary studies in that medium? What obligations does an institution have in supporting the improvement of their students' English skills? How can assessment practices be designed to enable students to demonstrate their knowledge and skills, independent of their language skills and in combination with them? What can institutions do to ensure that their graduates are prepared for professional roles and have achieved the graduate

English Language Standards in Higher Education

attributes they so willingly promote? How can institutions know whether they are achieving adequate levels of performance in each of these endeavours?

Higher education institutions that use English as the language of instruction and that host students from other linguistic backgrounds face these questions in their daily practice. Managing teaching and learning when some or all the student body has English as an additional language (EAL) poses unique challenges. Educators and administrators are called on to develop approaches that respond to these demands while they reflect on the particularities of the local context. In many cases their ability to do so is compromised by a lack of awareness of the options open to them. Higher education institutions have not viewed English language learning as a priority for policy and practice; not addressing this issue can disadvantage EAL students. A common view is that the onus of learning lies entirely with individuals, an approach that assumes it is a student's responsibility to ensure that their language skills are sufficient to engage in a particular area of study. Those who struggle are viewed as falling short. Among staff, impatience and irritation with students who fail to live up to expectations may result, and are likely to be particularly pronounced among those who have had little exposure to other languages themselves.

This deficit model of language learning assumes that those students who have gained the requisite grade in an approved English language examination should be able to cope with the demands of their studies, and ignores the multiple layers of discipline-specific discourse with which even a relatively fluent English language speaker may struggle. It refutes the notion that language skills require ongoing input and development if they are to improve. It is important to acknowledge that over the past two decades, higher education institutions have invested significant resources to develop language support programs for the growing numbers of EAL students, particularly international EAL students. All Australian higher education institutions now have, for example, a learning skills unit of some kind that offers language and academic skills support, although these resources remain marginalised and under-resourced, tangential to the curriculum rather than centralised.

Many academics and managers earnestly wish to support students whose language skills act as an impediment to full engagement with their studies. Their ability to do so is compromised by a lack of certainty of the best way to support EAL students. Disciplinary teaching staff, for example, may be unsure of the best way to fulfil their roles as educators and to facilitate students gaining the English language skills and knowledge their studies demand of them. There is often a lack of awareness of good practice and of successful initiatives in other institutions. Attempting to use innovations that have not been tried and tested can be risky for teaching staff in terms of resistance among students and negative feedback on the ever-important quality of teaching evaluation scores. Some staff may feel unsupported by institutional policies and structures that appear to prioritise the recruitment of students, and then fail to acknowledge responsibilities in their care.

Ensuring that all students are supported to optimise their learning is one of the fundamental roles of higher education institutions. The provision of quality education demands that institutional policies are innovative in responding to the needs of students from a whole range of backgrounds. Of significant concern is the evidence that students whose first language is other than English are struggling to learn; for example, that three years of study in an English-medium higher education institution does not always improve the English skills of students (Birrell 2006). This evidence indicates the need to rethink institutional practices. Fundamentally, ensuring that support for English language improvement is centralised in the curriculum is becoming increasingly essential.

In this book we address the issues raised for higher education institutions when they are using English to teach students for whom English is not their first language. Drawing on evidence from research with students and staff at a number of Australian higher education institutions we consider each of the key challenges in turn and provide both evidence-based insights and suggestions for teaching and management practices. The book provides a resource for those who need to make decisions about how institutions respond to the challenges raised, as well as for those whose professional responsibilities include teaching students. The book will resonate with higher education policymakers, administrators, leaders and teachers in all situations in which teaching is conducted in English and some or all of the students taught are non-native English speakers.

The path to success

In many ways, the elevation of English as the international language in higher education has ensured that the ability to master its complexities has become a marker of success. Inequalities are exacerbated when some people are not only able to gain an education, but are also able to learn sufficient English to gain access to opportunities for social mobility, while others are unable to gain more than rudimentary schooling. The investment of time and effort in learning sufficient English to be able to function in a global context requires financial resources that are not available to many. Given the dominance of English, access to an array of opportunities and connections is privileged to those who have mastered its intricacies. Inevitably, the use of English in numerous professional situations ensures that attaining fluency in English has become one of the hurdles that aspirants need to clear. The subsequent encroachment of English into tertiary education is increasingly common. As Graddol (2006, p. 73) explains:

> Higher education is becoming globalised alongside the economy, and English is proving to be a key ingredient – partly because universities in the English-speaking world dominate the global league tables, and partly because English is proving popular as a means of internationalising both the student community and teaching staff.

One of the reasons that English proficiency has become so important to higher education derives from the power of multinational corporations. In 2010, CNN (CNN *Money* 2011) estimated that 176 of the world's top 500 companies had their headquarters in Europe and 139 in the USA, compared to 46 in China and 8 in India. Employment in a multinational company offers graduates opportunities and salaries that local firms struggle to match. In order to gain such sought-after positions, English proficiency is an absolute must. In 2005, McKinsey warned the Chinese of a 'looming shortage of home-grown talent' (Farrell & Grant 2005), suggesting that fewer than 10 per cent of Chinese graduates spoke good enough English to work in a multinational company. Of course not all graduates will be able to, or would want to, work in a multinational company. Nevertheless, the majority of organisations doing business in the 21st century conduct at least some of their activities transnationally, with many likely to have suppliers, contractors, clients and collaborators in a number of different countries. Their activities are likely to be conducted predominantly in English.

As a consequence of this demand, English is increasingly common as a language of instruction in higher education institutions around the world (Coleman 2006; Phillipson 2006; Tsui 2008). China's University and College Admission System (CUCAS) lists 32 Chinese institutions that offer English-medium courses in the field of business alone. Institutions in countries as diverse as Argentina, Israel, Russia, South Korea, Thailand and Turkey all offer full degree programs in the English language medium, as do institutions in most European countries (Study Abroad 2011). Even more countries have institutions that offer students the ability to study for part of a degree in English. Some programs are aimed at domestic students, commonly offering their expensive courses as a means of students gaining a global outlook as well as a degree, giving individuals a relative advantage over other graduates. Other programs specifically target international students, reflecting the demand for studying outside one's country of citizenship. In 2008, more than 3.3 million tertiary students enrolled in foreign institutions, the majority in English-speaking countries (OECD 2010), and it is likely that these numbers will only continue to increase in the future. By offering courses in English, higher education institutions in non-English-speaking countries are able to overcome their 'linguistic disadvantage in terms of attracting foreign students' (OECD 2008, p. 355) and tap into a highly lucrative market.

English language dynamics

The profusion of higher education institutions that offer education through the English medium to students from language backgrounds other than English demonstrates the way in which higher education institutions have been transformed by globalisation. Marginson and van der Wende (2009, p. 18) observe that higher education institutions have become 'mediums for a wide range of cross-border relationships'. As market forces have driven the explosion of contexts in which tertiary studies are conducted in the medium of English, and government policies ensure that students are more diverse in backgrounds and preparedness than ever before (Baldwin & James 2010; James, Krause, & Jennings 2010; Trow 2006), awareness of the implications for educational practice has lagged behind.

Not all students are required to pass an English language test prior to gaining entry to a higher education institution – the multiplicity of pathways means that students begin courses with differing levels of English language. If the entry level of students' English was regarded by institutions merely as a starting point for further development, this situation would not be overly problematic. Appropriate interventions and support would enable students to master the subject matter of their chosen area of study at the same time as improving their English proficiency. Ultimately, graduation would imply a double blessing: that they had achieved appropriate learning outcomes in a discipline and had improved their English skills to the level at which they could succeed in professional practice in the English-speaking world. For those choosing to engage in an international education, or to pay a premium to study at an English-medium institution in their own non-English-speaking country, such an outcome would justify the investment they and their families had made.

That these outcomes are not necessarily being achieved is indicated by the lament of employers unable to recruit graduates with sufficient English for employment (Arkoudis et al. 2009; Australian Education International 2010; Graduate Careers Australia 2008) and researchers who are raising doubts about whether higher education institutions are graduating students who have adequate levels of English for further study or for professional practice (Benzie 2010; Birrell 2006; Bretag 2007). Startling evidence from research conducted among students at Australian universities supports these findings. Research into the English language abilities of students who have spent three years in an English-medium institution are not reassuring. Birrell examined the results of more than 12 000 students applying for residency in Australia in 2005 and 2006 and found that one-third failed to achieve an overall band score of 6 in the International English Language Testing System (IELTS). This pattern was most pronounced among students from particular countries: more than 40 per cent of students from Bangladesh, Hong Kong, Korea, Nepal, Thailand and Taiwan gained an IELTS band score of 5 (Birrell 2006). It is highly unlikely that individuals with IELTS band scores below 6 have the fluency to function in professional situations. Birrell's findings sent shock waves ricocheting through the international education sector in Australia and generated significant controversy. Yet his use of raw quantitative overall band scores meant that little could be concluded about the stories behind each of the students he considered and whether there were differences in particular English language skills.

More recent research (O'Loughlin & Arkoudis 2009) used a more nuanced methodology that consisted of an analysis of IELTS band scores as well as questionnaires and interviews with student participants. Sixty-three students from the commerce faculty of an Australian higher education institution were recruited, half of whom were undergraduates and half of whom were coursework postgraduates. The students were from a number of Asian nations, including China, Malaysia and Indonesia. The IELTS band scores, which students had used for entry into their courses, were compared to results from a second IELTS test during the last semester of their courses. Forty-three students achieved an increase in their overall IELTS band score of 0.5 from their entry to exit test; 18 students received similar scores and two received a 0.5 lower band score in the exit test. Students' receptive reading and listening skills had improved more than their productive reading and writing skills. Any improvements in spoken English were not correlated to the other three dimensions. Students who had lower overall band scores at the start of their courses had experienced greater improvements than those with higher initial scores.

Some students demonstrated excellent improvements. One such student was Charmaine (pseudonym) who attributed the improvement in her English scores (from an overall IELTS band score of 6 to an overall IELTS band score of 7.5) to the fact that she had lived with an Australian host family throughout her studies, and that she had chosen to speak only English while in Australia, even with friends with whom she shared other common languages. Commenting on an acquaintance, she indicated that it was possible to succeed at an English-medium higher education institution without using English skills.

> He lives with five other Hong Kong people. He travels to university by driving. No communication. He lives in Box Hill, a very Chinese community. Over four years he got around not using much English. He did well at uni because his course is maths based.
>
> (O'Loughlin & Arkoudis 2009, p. 119)

Charmaine's comments about her friend are supported by (pseudonym) Daisy's experience. Daisy's overall band score in IELTS had remained the same, despite having spent almost three years studying in Australia; her writing score actually decreased by one band. Despite understanding the importance of improving her English skills, and her desire to seek employment in Australia, Daisy found it difficult to find people to speak English with, complaining that

> My friends always speak Chinese and I don't have the real environment to practise English. I can only read the newspaper and watch TV and I work in a hotel, but I'm doing accounting assistance, and working there helps (p. 121).

Daisy's limited opportunities to develop her English language ability were constrained by living with Chinese students, spending most of her time socialising with them and speaking Mandarin.

The experiences of Charmaine and Daisy demonstrate the multifaceted nature of a person's English skills and the processes that are vital to their improvement. Clearly, Charmaine actively positioned herself as a language learner, taking every possibility to improve her language skills. Daisy was less of a risk taker, which meant that she found opportunities to improve her English skills to be more limited. The different approaches taken by each student, and the environments in which they lived during their studies, resulted in very significant differences in English proficiency by the end of their degrees. The results indicate that English language development is neither predictable nor linear. They also suggest that different skills are developed in different ways. Crucially, the gains students made in speaking were attributed to activities outside of their studies, with few opportunities for discussions with other students or staff during classes. In contrast, those who sought support from academic units within the institution were more likely to improve their listening, reading and writing abilities. Those students who did not seek advice from academic units demonstrated fewer improvements. Taken together, these findings indicate a number of critical factors for English language improvement during higher education study. Clearly, not all students are the same, and it is likely that, in their social activities, unless students are risk takers they will fall back on the reassurance of familiar friends, their cultural communities and conversations in their native language. Providing support services is invaluable, but it does not help students who choose not to access these services. Each of these insights raises important questions that suggest the need to interrogate the way in which higher education institutions approach the teaching of students in the English medium when their first languages are not English.

Quality drives

Ensuring that all students achieve appropriate learning outcomes in their disciplines and have the communication skills necessary to succeed in their careers has commonly been determined under the auspices of internal institutional quality mechanisms, conceptualising quality as fitness for purpose (Woodhouse 2006). Higher education institutions have, historically, experienced high levels of autonomy in deciding whether students have met the standards required to be granted a degree in that institution, with little regulation by external agencies of curricula, assessments and student capabilities. This situation is one that is now undergoing review around the world in a dynamic revision of quality assurance in higher education. In some cases, this is occurring on a national basis. In Australia, the recent introduction of the Tertiary Education Quality and Standards Agency (TEQSA) indicates that a shift is taking place in the way in which tertiary education institutions are regulated, monitored and evaluated (Department of Education, Employment and Workplace Relations [DEEWR] 2011b). The coming of TEQSA has created much debate in Australia concerning what standards might mean as the sector transitions to mass and universal education (Gallagher 2010; R. James 2010).

As part of the changing architecture of Australian higher education, TEQSA oversees the My University website in which institutions are required to report a range of factors, including the results of student satisfaction surveys, measures of graduate skills, graduate outcomes, and quality of teaching and learning outcomes (DEEWR 2011a). While these figures have long been collected by institutions for internal use, this is the first time that they will be opened up to wider scrutiny. At the same time, a proportion of public funding for tertiary institutions will be based on the achievement of set performance targets. Overall, the level of scrutiny that institutions come under is set to rise significantly, adding a level of motivation for higher education institutions to ensure that all students are achieving their potential. As R. James (2010) states, this inevitably requires academic cultures to accept more transparency around academic standards, academic standard setting to be backed by robust assessment and grading approaches, and the need to consider public transparency as well as the regulatory aspects of academic standards.

Many national governments already provide guidelines to ensure that the provision of higher education to students who have English as an additional language is done according to quality principles. In illustration, the Australian government has developed 10 good practice principles for higher education institutions to follow in order to improve the English language proficiency of international students. The 10 principles are these:

1. Universities are responsible for ensuring that their students are sufficiently competent in the English language to effectively participate in their university studies.
2. Resourcing for English language development is adequate to meet students' needs throughout their studies.
3. Students have responsibilities for further developing their English language proficiency during their study at university and are advised of these responsibilities prior to enrolment.
4. Universities ensure that the English language entry pathways they approve for the admission of students enable these students to effectively participate in their studies.
5. English language proficiency and communication skills are important graduate attributes for all students.
6. Development of English language proficiency is integrated into curriculum design, assessment practices and course delivery through a variety of methods.

7 Students' English language development needs are diagnosed early in their studies and addressed, with ongoing opportunities for self assessment.
8 International students are supported from the outset to adapt to their academic, sociocultural and linguistic environments.
9 International students are encouraged and supported to enhance their English language development through effective social interaction on and off campus.
10 Universities use evidence from a variety of sources to monitor and improve their English language development activities.

(DEEWR 2009, p. 3)

The increased attention being paid to quality assurance strategies means that the way in which institutions address the needs of all students will be subject to ever greater examination. These developments will place English language standards in the spotlight as higher education institutions will need to make explicit their teaching and learning standards for English language development.

National developments are proceeding alongside, and mirroring, international developments. Drawing on the worldwide uptake of the Programme for International Student Assessment (PISA) scheme for measuring the extent to which 15-year-old secondary students are equipped to participate fully in society, the Organisation of Economic Cooperation and Development (OECD) is conducting a feasibility study into the Assessment of Higher Education Learning Outcomes (AHELO) at the tertiary level (Coates & Richardson 2011). AHELO is developing assessments to measure whether students have achieved the skills and knowledge required to function as professionals in their given fields. These assessments are being developed for use in a number of countries, with the strict translation protocols used in PISA used to ensure cross-national comparability. While starting in just two disciplines (economics and civil engineering), the potential for AHELO to spread to a wider range of disciplines, and to become entrenched in the quality assurance of higher education institutions around the world, is very great indeed.

In combination with a range of other methods for measuring and comparing curricula, institutional practices and student learning (including the Tuning Process and U-Multirank), these developments indicate that a growing onus is being placed on institutions to demonstrate that they can successfully facilitate student learning. The importance of ensuring that students achieve successful learning outcomes is paramount, whether or not the language of instruction is the same as the first language. The decision of the Russian Federation to use English language assessments with those students who are studying in the English language at Russian institutions during the qualitative testing phase of the AHELO Feasibility Study (Coates & Richardson 2011) is testament to the need to ensure that students educated in English can demonstrate their capabilities in English. This sets high standards for educational practice and demands that institutions meet their responsibilities towards students for whom English is an additional language. While some may argue that English assessment is currently included within the graduate attributes of higher education institutions, there is much variation across institutions: graduate attributes and desired learning outcomes are often unevenly embedded within the assessed curriculum (R. James 2010). As a result, while many institutions include English within their graduate attributes, usually in terms of effective communication skills in writing and speaking, what remains less clear is the extent to which disciplinary teaching and assessment practices include English language learning outcomes. Institutions currently appear to lack an agreed means by which to monitor and evaluate students' English language skills.

Premise of English language standards in higher education

This book advances debates about the role of higher education institutions in ensuring that EAL students graduate with the necessary English language skills for use in the workplace or further study. In doing so, we use a process approach to holistically consider the pathways of students and investigate their entrance, experience, exit and preparation for employment. In framing our analysis and discussion, we use a developmental model of English language proficiency (ELP) that is illustrated below in Figure 1.1. The concept of an ELP developmental continuum was conceived with Kieran O'Loughlin in 2010.

English: The language of higher education

As the model indicates, we transcend the traditional focus on minimum entry standards and instead analyse the key concerns regarding English standards across the period from entry to exit. The model emphasises the ongoing importance of students developing their social communicative language ability before, during and beyond their higher education studies. It also draws attention to the number of focal points in English language development as students move through the continuum from entry to study and on to employment or further education. The model incorporates Bachman's (1990) view of communicative language ability, and is supported by research that explores the language learning needs of EAL students in higher education (Benzie 2010; Elder & O'Loughlin 2003; Hyland 2009; O'Loughlin & Arkoudis 2009).

Bachman's model of communicative language ability has had a powerful influence on English language testing and assessment around the world. According to Bachman (1990), communicative language ability includes three components: language competence, strategic competence and psychophysiological mechanisms. Language competence is broken down into these elements.

- *Grammatical competence*, which involves using spoken or written language at word and sentence level to communicate meaning. The focus is on language use that involves vocabulary, grammar and sentence structure level.

Entry
- *Readiness to commence higher education study*
- ELP as general academic and social communicative language ability

Experience
- *Engagement with disciplinary teaching, learning and assessment tasks*
- ELP as specific (disciplinary) academic and social communicative language ability

Exit
- *Readiness to enter profession and/or further study*
- ELP as professional and social communicative language ability

Developed by O'Loughlin & Arkoudis

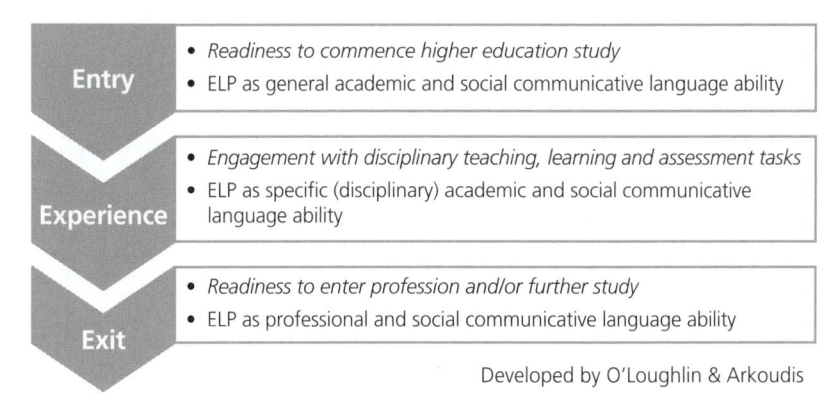

Figure 1.1: ELP developmental continuum

English Language Standards in Higher Education

- *Textual competence*, which centres on how phrases and sentences are joined together to form cohesive spoken or written texts. The focus is on language use at the discourse level.
- *Illocutionary competence*, which is concerned with the relationship between the words in the text and the intended meaning that the speaker or writer seeks to convey. The focus is on using language to express a wide range of meanings and to interpret the intended meaning of utterances or discourse.
- *Sociolinguistic competence*, which emphasises the control of the conventions of language use that are determined by the context within which the communication takes place. The focus is on the ability of the speaker or writer to communicate in ways that are appropriate within the particular context.

As Bachman explains, these factors constitute the 'what' of language testing or assessment. He views the four components of language competence as interrelated, and each is important when we consider students' English proficiency. Present within each component are the four language dimensions of listening, speaking, reading and writing. These dimensions consist of a range of separate and overlapping communication skills. A student might, for example, have a high overall proficiency with strong listening, reading and writing abilities but have only moderate speaking ability. Their overall proficiency might be reflected in strong written presentation skills but weak conversational skills.

Central to the issues discussed in this book that relate to entry and exit English standards is the role of English in disciplinary learning in higher education. We view English as integral to disciplinary learning. While students are required to meet minimum English standards to enter higher education institutions, they also need to demonstrate their understanding of disciplinary knowledge in written and oral presentations.

An individual's language ability combines their academic literacy and professional communication, and incorporates demands that evolve as they transition from enrolment, through teaching and learning in an academic environment, and on into professional employment or further study. As was stated above when outlining Bachman's view of language ability, it is difficult to separate academic literacy from professional communication, and we therefore use the broad term 'English language proficiency', or ELP, to define language ability. As such, academic literacy is one form of literacy required for success in higher education study and is a subset within the broader term of English language proficiency. In discussing ELP standards in higher education, the continuum of the student experience that involves ELP standards for entry to study, teaching and learning within a higher education context and exit into professional employment or further study need to be considered.

A shift in policies and practices is necessary in order to build a robust developmental model that will support students to improve their English skills. This would enhance and strengthen the current input-based model and enable higher education institutions to ensure that graduates have achieved sufficient English proficiency on completion of their degree. In order to achieve this, it is argued that a developmental approach to ELP is required where entry, teaching and learning and exit standards form a holistic and integrated view of ELP standards within higher education.

Structure of the book

In *English Language Standards in Higher Education* a chronological approach is taken to chart the passage of students from enrolment to exit, and to consider the issues that arise at each stage. Using data from a number of empirical studies with higher education students and teaching staff in Australia, the challenges and dilemmas that arise when higher education institutions teach English as an additional language students in the English medium (EAL) are considered. We then draw on our experience and expertise to recommend policies and practices that would address the needs that arise.

The chapters draw on the authors' recent research and experiences into English language proficiency (ELP) standards in higher education. In Chapter 2 some of the concern regarding ELP entry standards are raised and addressed. In Chapters 3, 4 and 5 issues related to embedding a developmental model of ELP within institutions are explored in detail. Chapter 6 explores ways that interaction between domestic and international students can be enhanced within teaching and learning contexts, and Chapter 7 discusses issues that relate to ELP development in offshore education. In Chapter 8 the influence of ELP on workplace readiness and employment outcomes of EAL students are examined. Each of these chapters refers to the key literature that relates to its theme, offers analysis of the key issues with some case study examples and draws out practical conclusions for policy and practice. The final chapter draws on the work presented in the book to offer suggestions for ensuring ELP standards in higher education.

Collectively, the following chapters engage with the complex issues involved in ELP standards and offer possibilities for addressing them through policy and practice. The complexities concerning ELP standards are presented in a manner that enables the discussion to be followed by a broad range of people who are interested in the issues presented in this book, including those not specifically involved in teaching or administering English language programs in higher education institutions. If progress is to be made on ELP standards in higher education, then the broader higher education community also needs to engage with the issues, and to consider possible suggestions for the future.

CHAPTER 2

ENGLISH LANGUAGE ENTRY STANDARDS

Higher education institutions place great importance on the academic credentials required of students before they can enrol. They are meticulous in setting academic entrance standards that ensure that prospective students have the ability to succeed with their studies. At the same time, they clearly understand that the skills and knowledge that entering students already possess are only a starting point, and carefully design curricula that enable students to develop their capabilities as they navigate their degrees. The role of teaching staff is to facilitate the progress and advancement of students throughout their higher education sojourn. Students are provided with significant support to build on what they bring with them on entry, enabling them to gain attributes that will help them to succeed in their future careers. Indeed, supporting students' learning and growth is one of the fundamental roles of higher education institutions.

Academic entrance standards are not the only requirements of students entering English-medium higher education institutions – they are also required to meet certain English language standards. Students with English as an additional language may take an English language subject in the final year of secondary school or they may enter via an alternative pathway. Some are required to demonstrate their English proficiency through taking an English language exam, while others are not. In many ways, higher education institutions do not approach the English language skills of EAL students with the same rigour they use for academic credentials. Among those higher education institution staff involved in admissions there is some confusion regarding the myriad pathways through which EAL students gain access to institutions and a limited ability to interpret the evidence students bring with them to demonstrate their language capabilities. Instead of viewing the improvement of the English skills of EAL students as something that they have a responsibility to support, institutions expect EAL students to have the required English language skills to be successful in their studies upon entry, tend to assume that automatic improvements will take place and do not consider it their responsibility to improve students' English skills.

In this chapter the standards that institutions set for the English language proficiency of incoming students and current practices in their application are considered. The chapter highlights the complexity of English language entrance requirements aimed at EAL students and considers the major role played by internationally recognised English language tests. We then focus on four major English language tests, including the International English Language Testing System (IELTS) and Test of English as a Foreign Language (TOEFL), paying particular attention to the differences between them. We question the reliance of institutions on such tests and highlight the care that needs to be taken in interpreting their scores, concluding with suggestions to guide institutional practices. Overall, we explore the readiness of students to commence higher education study – and question the extent to which current practices are effective in ensuring that EAL students succeed in their studies and are ready for employment on graduation. Suggestions for improving institutional practice in the selection of EAL students conclude the chapter.

Multiple pathways

The common assumption that all EAL students are required to gain a threshold score in a recognised English examination prior to entry to higher education is misleading. Instead, there are myriad pathways for EAL students to enter English-medium higher education institutions. Coley (1999), for example, identified a total of 61 kinds of evidence that were accepted at Australian higher education institutions as proof of English proficiency.

Some of the most common are English tests such as IELTS and TOEFL, entry via foundation programs or other tertiary studies, prior study in the English medium and length of residence in an English-speaking country. It is common for EAL students to take a circuitous route to higher education entry, navigating different education sectors, including English-medium secondary education, vocational education and training and English language intensive courses for overseas students (ELICOS). Research from Australian Education International (2007c), which tracked two cohorts of international students in Australia, found that almost one-third of students studied in more than one sector. Nineteen per cent of all international students moved from either ELICOS or vocational education and training into higher education. Others moved through a number of sectors to arrive in higher education. The routes taken by students tend to vary according to their nation of origin. Australian Education International found that those most likely to arrive in the higher education sector via ELICOS were from China, Hong Kong, Japan, Korea and Thailand. In contrast, those who entered higher education via vocational education and training tended to be from India. While use of the multiple pathways model is particularly true of Australia, Adams et al. (2009) contend that this approach is increasingly spreading internationally.

The presence of multiple pathways into higher education has many positive consequences. It enables EAL students to gradually build up their English language competence through studies that specifically target their English skills (such as ELICOS) as well as studies in less academically demanding courses (such as vocational education and training), or those that are intended to prepare students for university studies (foundation programs). The drawback is that not all pathways into higher education involve students needing to provide evidence of their English skills and, as O'Loughlin and Murray (2007, p. 10) point out, 'In many instances, international students may not be required to undertake a formal test of their English level prior to entry into their course of study'. This is commonly based on the assumption that study in ELICOS or vocational education and training for a set period inevitably results in an improvement in English skills, which automatically renders students ready for university studies. This is not necessarily the case: students who enter higher education institutions after a time in another type of educational institution, whether vocational education and training, ELICOS or a foundation studies course, are not required to provide evidence that their English is of a sufficient standard to cope with higher education studies.

It is unclear how EAL students who gain access to their higher education studies without having to take an English language test first fare in comparison to those whose English is tested. Research tends to be restricted to small-scale studies of students at specific institutions, which limits the ability to make generalisations. Moreover, the research that has been done indicates contradictory findings. Fiocco (2006) finds that students who enter higher education via pathways perform academically as well as others and have higher retention rates. In contrast, Hawthorne (2007) reports that students coming from foundation programs into a medical degree at one Australian institution underperform compared to students who enter via all other routes. Similarly, Fox (2005) finds that EAL students who are admitted to higher education on the basis of study in an English-medium secondary school perform less well than other EAL students. It is likely that the specific route that students take into higher education, and their prior experience with English, cause outcomes to vary. Without further research it is not clear whether the existence of multiple pathways for EAL students to enter into higher education should be viewed as enhancing opportunities and supporting language improvement or enabling those with inadequate English to fly under the language radar, negatively affecting their ability to cope with their studies. It is therefore important for staff to monitor the performance of students who enter via different routes and to take corrective action if problems arise. One way of doing so would be to require all students to take an English language examination prior to enrolment. But as discussed below, an overreliance on English language testing is not a panacea and can introduce new problems for institutions.

English language tests

Many higher education institutions around the world set minimum English language requirements for those EAL students who wish to enrol in a course, requirements that are additional to meeting the minimum academic requirements set for each course of study.

While individual institutions set their own entry requirements, there are high levels of convergence in the approaches they take, not only within countries but also across them. In countries such as Australia, no further sources of information are sought, while in other locations (such as the USA) additional indicators, such as personal references and the Scholastic Aptitude Test (SAT) results, are also taken into consideration (Van Nelson, Nelson, & Malone 2004). There are a number of English language tests available. They are generally proficiency tests. The objective of a proficiency test is predictive and it measures an individual's general ability. This means that they measure, as Davies et al. (1999, p. 154) clarify, 'how much of a language someone has learned', rather than being 'based on a particular course of instruction'. When discussing the English language in relation to higher education students, proficiency can be defined as 'the ability of students to use the English language to make and communicate meaning in spoken and written contexts while completing their university studies' (DEEWR 2009). We will now consider four of the main internationally used English language tests.

The International English Language Testing System (IELTS) Academic module is one of the more common ways for prospective students to demonstrate their English proficiency and is marketed as 'the world's proven English test' (IELTS 2011a). Until recently the IELTS Academic test, which is owned by the British Council, Cambridge ESOL Examinations and IDP Education, has been highly dominant for entry to higher education in the UK and Australia. Another Cambridge ESOL test is known as the Certificate in Advanced English (CAE). The CAE, which is one of the Cambridge suite of exams, is somewhat different to IELTS. Candidates generally undertake a 12-week preparation course in advance of the test, meaning that it is in some ways an achievement test rather than a proficiency test. The CAE is marketed as 'a high-level language qualification in English for demanding professional and academic situations' (University of Cambridge ESOL Examinations 2011a) and, while longstanding, has only relatively recently become recognised for entrance to higher education.

In a case of trans-Atlantic rivalry, the main alternative to the IELTS and CAE is the Test of English as a Foreign Language (TOEFL), owned by US company Educational Testing Services.

TOEFL has long been highly dominant in North America and is marketed as 'Your passport to study abroad' (Educational Testing Service 2011b). Another US organisation, in this case Pearson, owns the Pearson Test of English Academic (PTE Academic). Launched in 2009, this test, a relative newcomer to the market, is in a process of establishing its market niche.

As the interest in international study increases around the world, the market for each of these tests is significantly growing. It is likely that other tests will enter what is an extremely lucrative market sector. While nations and institutions have long tended to prefer one test over the others, this situation is now changing. The 2011 announcement by the Australian government that IELTS would no longer enjoy its near monopoly but would instead need to take its place alongside TOEFL, PTE and CAE (Department of Immigration and Citizenship 2011) is illustrative of the increasingly complex English language testing context. For institutions, the greater diversity of English tests is likely to make determinations about suitable English requirements for particular courses of study ever more challenging. Comparing different English language tests is a complex activity. Each one defines the language constructs they are measuring differently, and the highly competitive marketplace for English language tests ensures that test developers are unwilling to cooperate on studies to examine equivalency. To add to the complexity, each test is scored differently and allocates different amounts of time to the assessment of language skills. Some are deployed on paper and assess spoken English through face-to-face interviews, whereas others are deployed by computer and spoken English is assessed afterwards.

Moreover, there are variations in how each language area is assessed. The IELTS and CAE, for example, use interviews to assess spoken English; in the IELTS this involves one examiner and one candidate, whereas in CAE it involves two examiners and two or three candidates. In each case the tasks that students are required to undertake are different and the uses of language that they are assessed on are quite distinct. In the IELTS test, candidates are required to do three activities: respond to direct questions from the examiner about themselves, prepare and speak about a topic based on a prompt, and discuss abstract issues with the examiner (IELTS 2007). The IELTS speaking test lasts between 11 and 14 minutes and is conducted by a single examiner who interacts with the candidate and assesses their speaking ability. In the CAE, candidates take the speaking test with one or two other candidates, who are required to have a short conversation with the interlocutor about themselves, to use visual stimuli to give opinions, compare elements and speculate, and to work with other candidates to complete a collaborative task (University of Cambridge ESOL Examinations 2011a). In this case, the test lasts 15 to 18 minutes and is conducted by two examiners, one acting as an interlocutor, the other silently observing and assessing the spoken English of the candidates. The number of differences in the way in which spoken English is examined in the IELTS and CAE tests, and the fact that they are both developed by the same testing agency, provides just one indication of the complexity in comparing test scores.

Despite the difficulty in comparing test scores, this is something that institutional staff are required to do if they are to manage the enrolment of EAL students in a context in which more than one test score is accepted. Given the absence of a rigorous equivalency study of the scores between the four tests under discussion here, it is informative to consider a summary of their similarities and differences.

Table 2.1 brings together evidence from a number of sources to present a summary of the format of four English proficiency tests. It highlights the timing of each module, the way in which results are reported and the available scores. Given the complexity of each test, and the variations between them, it is important to read more about the specifics of each test in order to gain a full understanding of their scope and intent.

Some of the key differences between the four tests to take note of include the amount of time spent in testing the individual elements (assessment of reading in the TOEFL iBT takes double the amount of time of PTE Academic), the division of different elements (PTE Academic combines speaking and writing into one component, whereas the other three tests divide them into separate components), the way in which results are reported overall (TOEFL scores are an accumulation of scores from the different elements, whereas for the three other tests overall scores are means) and the complete contrast in methods of reporting English proficiency (IELTS uses a scale of 1 to 9, CAE uses A, B or C).

Table 2.1: Overview of four English tests

Test	IELTS Academic Module	TOEFL iBT	PTE Academic	CAE
Full name	International English Language Testing System (Academic module)	Test of English as a Foreign Language (iBT)	Pearson Test of Academic English	Cambridge English Certificate in Advanced English
Delivery	paper, and face-to-face interview	TOEFL iBT – internet-based test TOEFL PBT – paper-based test	computer	computer or paper and face-to-face interview
Speaking (minutes)	11–14	20	77–93	15
Writing (minutes)	60	50		90
Reading (minutes)	60	60–100	32–41	75
Listening (minutes)	30	60–90	45–57	40
Use of English (minutes)	–	–	–	60
Result reporting – overall	Overall band score (mean)	Total (cumulative)	Overall score (mean)	Grade and score (mean)
Result reporting – sub scores	Listening Reading Speaking Writing	Listening Reading Speaking Writing	Communicative skills (listening, reading, speaking, writing) Enabling skills (grammar, oral fluency, pronunciation, spelling, vocabulary, written discourse)	Listening Reading Speaking Use of English Writing
Score range	1–9	0–120 310–677	10–90	A–C and 0–100

Source: Educational Testing Service 2011b; IELTS 2011a; Pearson 2011b; University of Cambridge ESOL Examinations 2011a

Understanding test scores

The Council of Europe's Common European Framework of Reference (CEFR) for Languages (2004) defines six common reference levels in language ability: two basic levels, A1 (Breakthrough) and A2 (Waystage), two independent levels, B1 (Threshold) and B2 (Vantage), and two proficient levels, C1 (Effective operational proficiency) and C2 (Mastery). In regards to English for enrolment in higher education studies, levels B1, B2 and C1 are of greatest interest and will be considered below. To understand the great complexity involved in defining an individual's language ability it is instructive to consider the Council of Europe's description of language use (2004, p. 9).

> Language use, embracing language learning, comprises the actions performed by persons who as individuals and as social agents develop a range of competences, both general and in particular communicative language competences. They draw on the competences at their disposal in various contexts under various conditions and under various constraints to engage in language activities involving language processes to produce and/or receive texts in relation to themes in specific domains, activating those strategies which seem most appropriate for carrying out the tasks to be accomplished. The monitoring of these actions by the participants leads to the reinforcement or modification of their competences.

As this description indicates, assessing language ability involves reference to the context in which language is used, the objectives users are trying to achieve, the actions they undertake to achieve those objectives and the knowledge and skills they make use of. As may be expected, each of the terms used in the Council's description can be broken down into a number of constituent parts. Adding to the complexity is the fact that different people have different linguistic abilities, and language learning is highly contingent upon individual characteristics. As such, as the Council of Europe (2004, p. 17) acknowledges, 'Any attempt to establish "levels" of proficiency is to some extent arbitrary'.

Despite the complexities involved, the CEFR does delineate the global scales for each of the six levels of competency it defines; these are reproduced in Table 2.2. Once again, attention here will be limited to the three levels most relevant to EAL students in the higher education context. It is important to note that these are very generalised descriptions, so it is worth reading the detailed description of each discrete language element – listening, reading, spoken interaction, spoken production and writing – for greater insight into the level of language proficiency that each reference level refers to, as well as the ways in which the parts of each element are described. Spoken language, for example, is divided into range, accuracy, fluency, interaction and coherence.

The CEFR reference levels are useful for institutional staff in understanding English language test scores of students who wish to enrol in higher education courses for two key reasons. First, they have gone through a very long period of iterative development that has involved consultation with language experts in a wide number of

Table 2.2: Examples of Common European Frame of Reference global scales

Reference level	Global scale
C1 – Effective operational proficiency	Can understand a wide range of demanding, longer texts and recognise implicit meaning. Can express themselves fluently and spontaneously without much obvious searching for expressions. Can use language flexibly and effectively for social, academic and professional purposes. Can produce clear, well-structured, detailed text on complex subjects to show controlled use of organisational patterns, connectors and cohesive devices.
B2 – Vantage	Can understand the main ideas of complex text on concrete and abstract topics, including technical discussions in students' field of specialisation. Can interact with a degree of fluency and spontaneity that makes regular interaction with native speakers quite possible without strain for either party. Can produce clear, detailed text on a wide range of subjects and explain a viewpoint on a topical issue giving the advantages and independent disadvantages of various options.
B1 – Threshold	Can understand the main points of clear, standard input on familiar matters regularly encountered in work, school, leisure, etc. Can deal with most situations likely to arise while travelling in an area where the language is spoken. Can produce simple connected text on topics that are familiar or of personal interest. Can describe experiences and events, dreams, hopes and ambitions, and give brief reasons and explanations for opinions and plans.

Source: Council of Europe 2004, p. 24

languages, that is, they are a legitimate reference for understanding language ability. Second, and of more practical relevance, test developers have created resources that map their test results to the CEFR levels. Not only does this enable greater understanding of what different scores mean, but it also enables a broad level of comparison between them.

As noted above, there has been no scientifically conducted study that enables us to understand the equivalency of the scores students can gain in the IELTS, TOEFL, PTE Academic and CAE tests. Nevertheless, the agencies behind each test do provide a means of understanding their test scores in relation to the CEFR Reference levels. While this is highly unscientific, it is the best means currently available to compare scores between the tests.

Table 2.3 brings together evidence from the IELTS Academic, TOEFL iBT, PTE Academic and CAE, as well as from the Council of Europe, to indicate how the scores from each test fit with the CEFR reference levels. It should be noted that B1 equates to a fail in the CAE test.

As Table 2.3 indicates, there is considerable breadth in the range of scores that equate to each of the CEFR reference levels. Level B2 Vantage relates to a TOEFL iBT score of between 87 and 109, an IELTS band score of between 6.5 and 7.5, a PTE Academic score of between 59 and 75 and a CAE score of between 45 and 59. This is in part a product of the fact that the CEFR reference levels themselves are generalised, and also because it is impossible to determine the precise equivalency of different test scores in the absence of a rigorous study. It also highlights the difficult position of those setting English language standards for access to higher education courses. Determining that a student with an IELTS band score of 7

Table 2.3: Comparing test scores

CEFR reference level	TOEFL iBT	IELTS	PTE Academic	CAE
C1 Effective operational proficiency	110–120	8–9	76–84	60–79
B2 Vantage	87–109	6.5–7.5	59–75	45–59
B1 Threshold	57–86	5.5–6.5	43–58	–

Source: Educational Testing Service 2011a; Pearson 2011a; University of Cambridge ESOL Examinations 2012

can gain access to a particular course of study, while a student who gains an IELTS band of 6.5 cannot, is a highly arbitrary judgement. A student with an overall band of 6.5 may actually have superior language abilities in some areas than the one who has a band score of 7. It is very difficult to make distinctions at this level of specificity, and each test has a certain confidence interval around each score point. Overall test scores are arrived at by combining or averaging scores from discrete tests measuring different skills. Consequently, assuming that one overall score has a particular meaning that another does not is misleading.

Predictive ability of English test results

While it is important for higher education staff to have a basic understanding of the meaning of different English language test scores, the reliance of institutions on IELTS, TOEFL and other test results to ascertain the level of English proficiency that a prospective student possesses raises a number of practical and ethical problems. As O'Loughlin (2011) points out, great care needs to be taken in the way in which exam results are interpreted; ideally, they should be just one in an array of sources of evidence used to predict an EAL student's likely ability to be able to succeed in an English-medium course. This is particularly the case for two reasons. The first is that there is little evidence that English language test scores predict an individual's ultimate success in an English-medium study environment. The second is that different courses of study have very different linguistic demands. Taken together, these factors ensure that placing great weight on a numerical test result, one that is already a composite of a number of discrete scores for different linguistic skills, is a risky business. Even so, it is an activity that admissions staff undertake on a regular basis.

English testing agencies are keen to promote the objectivity and authenticity of their tests and the fact that they are widely accepted by institutions around the world. They vigorously promote the methods used for scoring, the security of test items, the training of examiners and the rigour with which the tests have been created. Educational Testing Service suggests that students who perform well on the TOEFL iBT 'are prepared to do their best in the classroom and beyond' (Educational Testing Service 2011b, p. 6). Similarly,

IELTS states that the 'Academic reading and writing assess whether a candidate is ready to study or train in the medium of English at an undergraduate or postgraduate level' (IELTS 2007, p. 2). Equally, Pearson maintains that the PTE Academic test 'accurately assesses real-life academic English skills' (Pearson 2011b), while the CAE is marketed as 'the leading exam for professional and academic English' (University of Cambridge ESOL Examinations 2011a). While the rigour with which these tests are created is estimable, it is not at all clear that good performance on any of them is able to predict good performance in academic studies once an EAL student is accepted by an institution.

Significant research has been conducted to investigate whether it is possible to predict academic performance from English test results. The major difficulty in reaching a conclusion is that academic performance is influenced by a large range of factors, language proficiency being just one of them. Attempting to isolate the influence of an individual's English proficiency on their academic performance is, therefore, a difficult task. Bayliss and Ingram (2006) list a number of studies that have found positive links between IELTS band scores and the academic performance of students, and others that have not. They highlight the inevitable inconsistency in these findings. Lee and Greene (2007) concur, suggesting that factors such as students' background knowledge of and familiarity with the style of teaching are critical factors in determining academic success. Wait and Gressel (2009) suggest that the predictive validity of English test scores may be dependent on the field of study that students enter.

Without strong evidence that English language test results can accurately predict the academic performance of EAL students, perhaps the best conclusion that can be drawn is that any relationship is influenced by a host of additional factors. Nevertheless, there is evidence that the perception among students and teaching staff that English proficiency is of profound importance to academic success is widespread (Hyatt & Brooks 2009; Lee & Greene 2007). As we have seen, though, over-reliance on test results is risky. If higher education institutions are to ensure that all the EAL students they enrol have the English skills to be able to succeed with their studies, a nuanced and complex means of assessing English proficiency is clearly required. Ideally, institutions should seek broad evidence of

EAL students' English proficiency through the use of references, examples of written work and interviews to supplement English test results. In reality, the sheer volume of applicants and the magnitude of the enrolment process means that this is difficult to put into practice. At the very least, it is imperative that institutional staff understand that the use of a single test score to determine whether an individual has the English language skills to cope with a course of study is at best a very blunt tool. Caution needs to be taken in drawing conclusions from test scores, and effort is required to understand the very complex nature of language ability.

Setting English language requirements

If the purpose of a test is to measure a specific form of English, it must be designed to include tasks that prompt test takers to reproduce that form of English during the test. To do so, the nature of the form of English that is being tested must first be established. As Elder and Harding (2011, p. 34) note, 'The language construct … needs to be defined very carefully with respect to the particular situation or purpose for which the test is intended'. Thus, a test of English for accounting would begin with an analysis of the type of English used in higher education accounting curricula and the profession of accounting to enable a precise definition of the target language that needs to be tested. The test would be expected to include language, including accounting terminology, and tasks that closely correlate to the activities required of students during their studies and professional demands placed on accountants. In a well-designed test of English for accounting, those who perform well would be expected to also perform well in their accounting studies and in a professional accounting situation.

The problem with English tests such as the academic version of IELTS and PTE Academic is that 'academic' is a very broad term. Consequently, the very best that test developers can do is to define the general English that is required in academia. Given the vast array of disciplines, skills and capabilities encompassed in the term 'academic', any test of academic English is necessarily broadly relevant to a number of disciplines but not specifically relevant to any. As Lynch (2011) and Moore and Morton (2005) note, there are significant and important differences between the academic requirements of students at higher education institutions and the tasks they are required to complete during English tests. If writing tasks alone are considered, a test taker may be required to write an essay to debate the advantages and disadvantages of a particular issue when, as a mathematics student, this is not something they are likely to face during a degree. In contrast, a philosophy student may be required to interpret a bar graph when this is never likely to feature in a philosophy curriculum. Because test results do not indicate what kind of task a student has performed, it is not possible to know whether their good or poor performance will have any bearing on their future academic performance.

At the same time, fields of study vary in their linguistic demands. IELTS distinguishes between four types of study and highlights differing requirements for each one. In relation to 'linguistically demanding academic courses' such as medicine and law, for example, IELTS recommends that 7.5 is a minimum acceptable band score. In contrast, the minimum acceptable band score for entry to 'linguistically less demanding academic courses' such as agriculture, pure mathematics and technology is 7 (IELTS 2007). Crucially, IELTS notes that a significant burden rests on institutions to determine the appropriate minimum band score for entry to a particular area of study:

> Assessment of performance in IELTS depends on how the candidate's ability in English relates to the language demands of courses of study or training, not on reaching a fixed pass mark. The appropriate level required for a given course of study or training is ultimately something which institutions / departments / colleges must decide in the light of knowledge of their own courses and their experience of overseas students taking them (p. 5).

In reality, institutions tend not to use a nuanced approach to setting minimum language requirements for entry to particular courses. Instead, demands of simplicity in enrolment procedures dictate the use of a general minimum band score across all institutional offerings. Commercial considerations ensure that the English level of consumers dictates the band score used, with an IELTS overall band score of 6 or 6.5 most common of all. While scores such as these may be acceptable for students wishing to study

[English Language Standards in Higher Education

catering or pure science (IELTS 2007), without further study they are not adequate for more linguistically demanding courses. Many EAL students struggle to cope with their study quite simply because their limited English proficiency means that they should never have been allowed to enrol in the first place. This is a painful and self-evident truth that institutions are loath to admit. While many senior higher education staff do privately acknowledge the flaws in their enrolment of EAL students who have inadequate English skills, the pressures of attracting students in a competitive market are given as an excuse for such policies. As Hyatt and Brooks (2009) affirm, such tensions are increasingly common in a market-driven higher education sector.

Beyond failing to take account of the varying linguistic demands of different areas of study, institutional policies also fail to consider the specific language requirements of particular courses. It is easy to forget that band, total or overall scores represent either a composite or an average of discrete scores for particular language skills. As Table 2.1 illustrates, these include the receptive skills of listening and reading and the productive skills of speaking and writing. IELTS specifically indicates that it is important to consider the scores for each component in relation to the demands of a particular course. IELTS, for example, notes that 'If a course has a lot of reading and writing, but no lectures, listening comprehension might not be quite as important and a score of, perhaps, 5.5–6 in Listening might be acceptable if the Overall Band Score was 7' (IELTS 2007). Such nuance is rarely seen in higher education admission requirements, inevitably a result of the input required. Golder et al. (2009) report on establishing the IELTS band scores for admission to computer technology courses at a Canadian higher education institution. They ultimately determine that an overall band score of 6.5 is necessary, with 7 in reading and 6 in speaking. Noteworthy are the range of band scores they select and the considerable time and effort required to reach this conclusion. It is all too easy for institutional staff to find that determinations such as these fall to the bottom of the pile of competing demands on their time.

While it is easy to understand why shortcuts are taken in setting and interpreting English language test scores in the administration of enrolment procedures, doing so represents a missed opportunity. As Hyatt and Brooks (2009, p. 52) note, the individual component

32

scores on tests such as IELTS, TOEFL, PTE and CAE represent 'valuable information that could inform the admissions process'. Investing more energy and effort up front to make sure that all students enrolled into a higher education course have the ability – academic and linguistic – to succeed in their studies would save problems later on. Poor enrolment processes invoke complexities for institutions in dealing with struggling students and place an enormous burden on institutional staff. This burden can lead staff to regard EAL students as a problem, derailing institutional efforts at internationalisation and creating tensions between staff and students. At the same time, enrolling EAL students into courses for which their English skills are inadequate, and failing to provide them with sufficient support to remedy this situation, places individual students under significant stress, and can cause high levels of frustration and distress (Murray 2010).

The fault for each of these oversights does not lie with individual staff but rather with institutional policies. Hyatt and Brooks (2009) investigated the IELTS awareness of academics and admissions administrators at UK institutions. They found that the majority of those they surveyed were at best vague about the IELTS test and were unclear about what it measured or how it worked. This concurs with other research conclusions (see O'Loughlin 2011; Rea-Dickins, Kiely, & Yu 2007; Smith & Haslett 2007). At the very least such research findings suggest that if tests are to be used to measure the English levels of EAL students, those staff tasked with interpreting scores require training. Such training would need to incorporate a basic introduction to the elements that comprise the discrete scores, as well as a thorough understanding of the different test types and the relationship of their scores to institutional demands.

Overcoming the limitations of English language tests

As this chapter has made clear, it is very difficult for institutions to be sure that the EAL students they enrol have adequate English language skills to cope with their studies. This is true for a number of reasons. First, the existence of multiple pathways into study means that many EAL students are not required to take English tests prior to enrolment. Second, the increasing profusion of recognised English proficiency tests makes the tasks of interpreting test scores ever more difficult. This is particularly the case because different tests measure English proficiency in different ways. Third, there is inconsistent evidence that English proficiency tests are able to predict academic performance – there are simply too many other factors which affect the ability of EAL students to cope with their studies. Fourth, different areas of study and different methods of teaching require EAL students to have different strengths in particular language skills. Taken together, it is difficult for institutions to ensure that the enrolment mechanisms they use to control the admittance of EAL students are achieving their objectives.

The challenge of ensuring that EAL students can cope with the English demands of their studies is reinforced by the fact that language skills are neither static nor uniform. As the following chapters will discuss, ongoing language support and carefully designed assessment mechanisms are required to enable EAL students to continue to improve their English skills throughout their studies. To enable language improvements to be facilitated, it is first necessary to determine language needs. This is best done in the context of a particular area of study. As Wette (2011) argues, those with expertise in a particular area of study or professional practice are likely to assess language performance quite differently to how they assess mainstream English tests because they are aware of the contexts in which individuals will need to communicate and the tasks they will need to undertake. This indicates the need for English language experts and domain experts to work together collaboratively to create means of measuring the language needs of students in a particular area of study, and then ways in which improvements can be supported.

The focus on ongoing improvements is an important one. As is discussed in the following chapters, higher education institutions that recruit EAL students need to transcend an exclusive focus on entrance standards in order to consider a holistic and developmental model of support for EAL students throughout their studies. However well designed and nuanced English language requirements are, they can only ever indicate the preparedness of an individual student to commence a particular course of study. The complex nature of English language skills means that it is rarely possible to predict future academic performance from English language test scores. It is more helpful to assume that however well an EAL student performs on an English language test, they will require some degree of support throughout their degree if they are to graduate with optimal English language skills that will enable them to perform well in their chosen career. Achieving this outcome for all EAL students is not something that can be left to chance but instead calls for a carefully designed program of support, one that enables students to develop specific academic and social communicative skills. As quality assurance frameworks place ever greater demands on institutions to demonstrate that they are doing all they can to optimise their students' education, programs that support the English language skills of EAL students can no longer be considered luxuries and are certain to become an integral part of higher education activities.

Summary

There are a number of steps that higher education institutions and their staff can take to ensure that the enrolment of EAL students is managed in a way that optimises positive outcomes for students and institutions alike. Ideally, a nuanced, rather than broad brush, approach to the enrolment of EAL students, depending on the linguistic demands of particular fields of study, should be used. While this is highly advantageous it can cause administrative complexities. There are a number of steps that institutions can take to enhance the enrolment of EAL students.

- Admissions staff need to be aware of the multiple pathways into higher education study, and that not all involve thorough assessment of English language skills.
- Institutions may wish to consider requiring those students who enter via pathways in which their English proficiency is not assessed – such as foundation programs, vocational education and training courses and English-medium secondary schools – to take an English proficiency test prior to enrolment.
- Additional indications of English language proficiency, such as references, examples of written work and interviews, may be requested from students and used by institutions to complement English language proficiency test scores.

- All staff involved with setting and administering English language requirements for admission to higher education would benefit from training that provides them with an introduction to the components that comprise English language proficiency and the ways in which different tests attempt to measure these.
- Institutional staff need to be aware of the ways in which test scores from different English language proficiency tests – such as IELTS, TOEFL, CAE and PTE – relate to each other, and their correlation with the reference levels defined in the Common European Framework of Reference for Languages.
- Institutions may wish to work together to persuade testing agencies to conduct equivalency studies to create a better understanding of comparisons between scores from different tests.
- Institutions need to acknowledge that English language proficiency tests are limited in their predictive ability and that differences between an IELTS 6 and IELTS 6.5 score, for example, may be negligible in determining the ability of one student to cope with their studies and another to struggle.
- Institutions would be advised to establish processes to enable ongoing monitoring of student progress from different entry pathways in order to build up knowledge on the adequacy of entrance requirements for particular degree programs and to allow for the adjustment of these requirements where they are found to be inadequate.
- Rather than relying on test scores as proof that an EAL student possesses the English proficiency to succeed in their studies, institutions would do better to focus their attention on supporting ongoing English language improvement throughout their studies.
- It would be valuable for English language experts to advise staff in specific disciplines on the key demands of a course and the level of English language proficiency it demands. This may lead to setting specific English language requirements for different courses and/or determining the key areas in which EAL students are likely to require support.

CHAPTER 3

MODELS OF ENGLISH LANGUAGE PROGRAMS

English language support programs are one of a number of services made available to higher education students. They exist in many institutions where English is the medium of instruction and their traditional role has been to fix up any English language problems students may encounter during the course of their study. The main responsibility for students' English language proficiency (ELP) development resides within units and centres that offer academic language and learning support. Those working within such units increasingly collaborate with academic staff to address the language needs of EAL students within disciplinary teaching. This activity is not without its challenges.

In relevant literature a number of terms are used to refer to staff who support students with English as an additional language (EAL) to develop their English language skills for higher education. These terms include academic language and learning (ALL) advisers, language and academic skills advisers and English language specialists. In this book we prefer to use the term 'English language specialists' to identify the staff who work to address the language learning needs of EAL students. This is an inclusive term that incorporates ALL advisers who work closely with EAL students (not all members of ALL centres or units work with EAL students), as well as academics who are not attached to an ALL unit or centre but who work with EAL students. When we do refer to ALL advisers, we mean those who work with EAL students.

English language support programs have grown over the last 10 years in response to the growing numbers of EAL students attending English-medium higher education institutions and the increasing unease among academics about how to best address their language and learning needs. A number of different models are used by institutions in different countries. In the UK and Australia English language support programs can range from individual student consultations to English language specialists working with disciplinary staff (Arkoudis & Starfield 2007; Barthel 2011; Wingate 2007). Within the Asia–Pacific area, similar programs are available in institutions where English is the medium of instruction. The USA differs slightly from both the UK and Australia, in that all undergraduate students take freshman composition as a credit-bearing course. The diversity of approaches is reflective of the significant efforts made by institutions to find the best way to support their EAL students. One strategy in isolation is never likely to be as effective as a holistic approach. Research does, however, indicate that some models are more effective than others.

One challenge faced by English language support in institutions is how to reinvent their programs into those that focus on English language development rather than support. This is an important distinction, as the term 'development' captures an educative approach to English language learning and teaching, whereas the term 'support' tends to reinforce a deficit view of the student as lacking the necessary skills. English language support programs mainly developed in an era in which quality assurance was posited as fitness for purpose and the presence of a variety of support programs was adequate evidence that institutions were addressing the ELP needs of their students. Within the current climate of teaching and learning standards there is an imperative for institutions to ensure that graduates have attained the required ELP learning outcomes, or standards, for the workplace or further study. As such, it is important for them to consider the number of possible strategies that exist and the best way for these to be integrated into an overall course of study. In this chapter, the different models of English language support that exist will be explored and some of the key challenges they face will be identified.

Models of practice

This section provides an overview of the number and variety of English language support programs offered in Australian higher education institutions. It presents data available from the Association for Academic Language and Learning (AALL) website (Barthel 2011), which summarises information regarding the professional practices that academic language and learning centres and units within Australian institutions engage in. This information is mapped onto a framework developed by Jones, Bonanno and Scouller (2001) for categorising models of collaboration of ALL practices. The aim of this mapping activity is to scope, in very broad terms, the practices in Australian institutions and to identify levels of collaboration between English language specialists and disciplinary academic staff.

According to Barthel (2011), all 39 Australian universities have at least one ALL unit or centre. Central units or centres offer academic language and learning support to all students and work with disciplinary staff across the institution. Of the 39 universities, about 18 have faculty-based ALL centres that work with students in those faculties, mainly in faculties where there are large numbers of EAL international students, such as business and medicine. In 2011, 500 full-time tenured ALL staff were employed in Australian universities, and Barthel has estimated that more than half of such staff are classified as academic, which, in Australia, means that they conduct and publish research as well as teach students, much like the disciplinary academics in universities.

The AALL funded a project to survey ALL centres and units in relation to the variety of practices that they offered within their universities in 2008. This database was updated in November 2011, allowing an indication of the activities which were becoming increasingly common. Table 3.1 presents a summary of the main activities, a general definition used to categorise the ALL activities for the AALL database and the number of universities where particular activities operated in both 2008 and 2011.

As Table 3.1 indicates, between 2008 and 2011 the number of ALL activities has generally increased. Although the table provides general and broad information about a number of ALL practices, it would seem that the largest number of increased activities are in the generic non-credit workshops (11 universities), followed

Table 3.1: Academic language and learning activities in Australian universities

ALL activity	Definition	Number of Australian universities (2008) n=39	Number of Australian universities (2011) n=39
Integrated credit	Discipline-specific credit bearing subject(s)/units embedded within courses, sometimes compulsory; usually owned by faculties and frequently co-developed/co-taught by ALL and faculty staff.	13	20
Integrated non-credit	Discipline-specific non-credit subject(s)/units or workshops embedded within courses, normally non-compulsory, usually developed/taught by ALL staff.	26	34
Generic credit	Non-discipline-specific credit bearing subject(s) (for example, Essay Writing 101, English for Academic Purposes), sometimes compulsory, usually available to all students, often as electives, owned by faculties or ALL units and usually developed or taught by ALL staff.	13	16
Generic non-credit	Non-discipline-specific non-credit bearing courses/workshops, usually available to all students, usually owned by ALL units and usually developed/taught by ALL staff.	28	37
Support for research students	ALL courses and workshops available specifically to postgraduate research students.	30	34
One-to-one consultations with students	Individual appointments and/or drop-in services/facilities.	38	38
Educational development	ALL educators involved in curriculum and/or staff development activities with faculty staff.	26	34
English as a Second Language (ESL) tuition	Provision of ESL support to enrolled students (mainly international) with limited (below required IELTS) English proficiency.	16	24
Diagnostic assessment	Post-enrolment language assessment of student cohorts.	18	27

Source: Adapted from Barthel 2011, p. 1

by post-enrolment language assessment, integrated non-credit workshops and English as a second language tuition specifically designed for EAL students. Seven universities reported increased activities in integrated credit subjects and educational development, highlighting the increased attention given by universities to these activities, although only 20 universities had integrated credit subjects. Nearly all Australian universities offer one-on-one consultations and generic non-credit workshops. These more traditional approaches to supporting EAL students are also the ones where there is very little evidence of students' ELP learning outcomes.

Individual consultations

Individual consultations involve English language specialists providing feedback to students on work that will be assessed by academics. The aim of these sessions is to develop students' academic writing abilities. While there is very little research that investigates the effectiveness of individual consultations for student learning, the studies that have been conducted indicate there are some positive outcomes for English language specialists. Chanock (2007a) has presented a strong set of arguments for maintaining individual consultations because what she gains from these consultations is insights that she is able to share with academics and larger groups of students about the English language difficulties international students encounter during their studies. Woodward-Kron (2007), through a detailed analysis of the interactions between a learning skills adviser and an international postgraduate student, concludes that while there is some evidence that individual consultation has potential for scaffolding student learning, it is also a very time-consuming process. She argues that consultations can play an important role in students' writing development but emphasises that there are 'divisive conflicting perspectives and issues associated with individual consultation' (p. 13). These issues particularly relate to the difficulty of separating language learning from disciplinary teaching and learning. Although, ideally, English language specialists would offer feedback on student consultations with disciplinary academics, it is very difficult to find the time for this approach to take place. There are also cost issues for higher education institutions in which hundreds of students require support and each student may need a number of sessions. In other words, individual consultations are a very costly approach to offering support and there is very little evidence that this support leads to students developing their English language proficiency skills.

Workshops

Workshops are a popular model of English language support in higher education institutions and can range from focusing on generic to discipline-specific English language teaching. Generic workshops cover areas such as oral presentations, academic writing and developing conversational skills. Discipline-specific workshops can often include a focus on developing academic reading and writing in particular disciplines.

A number of issues have thrown into doubt the effectiveness of this model of English language development. Attendance at workshops is generally voluntary, a critical issue with these programs (Arkoudis & Starfield 2007; Wingate 2006). Consequently, only the most motivated students attend, often those least in need of support. Students do not necessarily consider attending workshops a priority in their study program (O'Loughlin & Arkoudis 2009). Many EAL international students from China consider it more appropriate to ask their lecturer or tutor for assistance because for them learning is embedded in the discipline and not with external support services (Watkins 2007).

Anecdotal and research-based evidence suggest that some of the EAL students who require support do not attend workshops because they are struggling to meet the demands of their enrolled subjects (Kingston & Forland 2008). While some academic language and learning units report that international students with English as an additional language are over-represented as a percentage of the total student population, for the reasons stated above it appears that workshops may not necessarily be attracting those international students who are most in need of English language support.

This inconsistency in attendance makes it difficult to develop a workshop program that has any continuity for developing English language abilities. Research indicates that English language development is complex (Ellis 1997). Elder and O'Loughlin (2003) found that students who enrolled in presessional English language courses managed to increase their IELTS score by an average of 0.5 over a 12-week period of intensive instruction, although this was not the case for all students. Indeed, it appears that proficiency increases are slower once students reach the upper bands of IELTS proficiency scores. Studies have also shown that while EAL international students overcome some of their difficulties with listening, reading and speaking abilities in the first two years of their undergraduate course, academic writing across the different disciplines can remain a problem for these students throughout the three years of their degree (Zhang & Mi 2010). This raises an important issue regarding the extent to which English language support workshops can develop students' English language proficiency, given that academic writing within the disciplines is the main form of assessment in higher education and that problems in this area can persist for students for the entirety of their undergraduate degree.

Collaboration with disciplinary academics

While Table 3.1 highlights the variety of activities that academic language and learning centres or units are involved in, of particular interest for the discussion in this chapter are the levels of collaboration between English language specialists and disciplinary academics, as one of the main challenges lies in repositioning English language as development rather than support.

In examining collaborative practices, Jones et al. (2001) found that different models can operate within institutions. They structured these from weak forms of collaboration, such as weak adjunct activities, through to strong models of collaboration that include embedded activities. Here, their categories are presented in order from weak to strong levels of collaboration.

- *Adjunct* (disciplinary context is weak), in which workshops are offered outside of the students' scheduled classes. Included in this category are the generic workshops, in which there is little collaboration between English language specialists and disciplinary academics, even though workshops may be conducted within faculties.
- *Adjunct* (disciplinary context is strong), in which workshops are designed for a specially targeted group of students. The focus of teaching may be on writing in a specific genre or preparing an oral presentation.

- *Integrated*, in which workshops support the development of English language proficiency within disciplinary teaching and learning. It is usually delivered by English language specialists and timetabled into students' courses.
- *Embedded*, an approach that refers to collaborative design of a curriculum in which development of English language proficiency is incorporated within the teaching. It usually involves English language specialists and disciplinary academics working together to plan the teaching, learning and assessment tasks. The academic usually teaches the material; team teaching can also be involved.

Jones and her colleagues stress that, within the models, many variations exist and that different contexts require different approaches to the types of models that operate within an instuttion. They emphasise that it is not necessary to aim exclusively for embedded approaches; their experiences have indicated that it is difficult to sustain such programs for more than two years.

The activities outlined by Barthel (2011) have been mapped onto the four main models identified by Jones et al. (2001), as demonstrated in Table 3.2. The main criterion used to classify the activities was whether they facilitated collaboration between English language specialists and disciplinary academic staff. With most activities, such as generic non-credit workshops, there was little ambiguity in terms of classification. However, based on the available data, the activity 'support for research students' was difficult to classify as this activity included general, discipline-specific integrated and non-integrated. In this case, the activity was left out of the table, as it could be included in all models of collaboration.

Table 3.2: Models of collaboration

Model of collaboration (Jones et al. 2001)	Academic language and learning practices (Barthel 2011)
Adjunct weak	Generic credit (16)
	Generic non-credit (37)
	One-to-one consultations (38)
Adjunct strong	English as a second language tuition (24)
Integrated	Integrated non-credit (34)
Embedded	Integrated credit (20)

Table 3.2 shows that higher education institutions offer a range of activities to support language learning. Most Australian institutions have integrated non-credit subjects, in which workshops are linked to disciplinary learning. While there have been shifts towards stronger models of collaboration, most program options are within the adjunct weak models of collaboration. This poses certain challenges in terms of ensuring graduates' English language standards. The voluntary attendance of weak adjunct models means that it is difficult to develop students' proficiency. These programs offer a service to students who may need to understand how to structure an essay or the correct use of referencing, but in comparison with more integrated models there is little research about the English language learning of weak adjunct models.

While policy and research emphasise the importance of developing collaborative practices between academic language and learning staff and disciplinary academics, this can be difficult to achieve. As Chanock (2007b, p. 272) has stated:

> [Academic language and learning staff] are chronically frustrated by the difficulty of sharing what we learn from our students with the people who are teaching and marking them. In order for such sharing to take place, however, some obstacles – both structural and cultural – would need to be overcome.

We have identified three main obstacles for collaboration between academic language and learning staff and disciplinary academics. These are

- hierarchy of disciplines within higher education
- transition from elite to mass to universal education
- status of academic language and learning staff.

Hierarchy of disciplines within higher education

According to Reid (1992), curriculum as institution and curriculum as practice are important in legitimising the standing of a discipline within the practices of a higher education institution. Curriculum as institution means that the discipline embodies what is tested, useful, necessary for courses to teach, accountable and relevant to society more broadly. Curriculum as practice refers to the teaching, learning and assessment activities that constitute the subject. Reid does not propose a dichotomy between curriculum as institution and curriculum as practice. Rather, he emphasises that both areas need to be taken into account. Disciplinary curriculum as institution, for example, refers to grading, examining and maintaining disciplinary traditions; the claims of disciplinary curriculum as practice involve selecting the particular content to teach and developing approaches to teaching and learning.

In recent years, with the increase in accountability for teaching and learning in higher education, the focus for most disciplines has been on developing curriculum as practice. Academic language and learning as a discipline has struggled in terms of institution and practice. In Australia, ALL activities began around 30 years ago, mainly as a clinical model of support and offering 'remedial' activities to address the problems that students were encountering with their academic work (Stevenson & Kokkinn 2009). While ALL activities have evolved since those early years, ALL is lower within the hierarchy of disciplines compared to areas such as medicine, law, arts and science.

In terms of curriculum as institution and practice, ALL advisers do not have a high profile within the practices of institutions. It is unclear what the nature of the ALL discipline is within institutions. One of the main problems appears to be that the ALL 'body of knowledge remains unclear to the rest of the academy' (Velautham & Picard 2009, p. A131). It would appear that, to a certain extent, ALL activities lack the same legitimacy that other disciplinary subjects have within institutions and this can create barriers in developing communities of practice with disciplinary academics, largely because ALL staff are often positioned as operating 'at the margins of academic life' (Chanock 2007b, p. 273).

Elite to mass to universal education

Since the Second World War, higher education institutions have slowly moved from elite to mass to universal access. Trow (2006, p. 243), in his revisit to his 1973 paper, defines the three stages as

> elite – shaping the mind and character of a ruling class, a preparation for elite roles; mass – transmission of skills and preparation for a broader range of technical and economic elite

roles; and universal – adaptation of the 'whole population' to rapid social and technological change.

Trow emphasises that these three stages of access are not distinct phases. He argues that higher education institutions do not transition as a whole from an elite to a mass phase, but rather that aspects of elite and mass education remain within institutions as they move towards universal access. As he explains:

> The analysis of the phases of development of higher education should not be taken to imply that the elements and components of a system of higher education can change at equal rates, and that a system moves evenly toward the characteristic forms of the next phase. In fact, development is vey uneven; numerical expansion may produce a more diversified student body before the curriculum has been similarly diversified; the curriculum may become more diversified before the recruitment and training of staff has changed to meet the new requirements of the changed curriculum (2006, p. 265).

In terms of the role of English language in higher education, the moves towards universal education, the increasing numbers of students with English as an additional language and the widening participation agenda in higher education has meant that these students arrive for study with different educational experiences from those expected from students beginning study in an elite phase. Yet, as they have met the institutional entry requirements, students are perceived by many academics as entering higher education with the necessary level of English language proficiency. Addressing ELP problems is regarded by many academics as mechanical (Chanock 2007b) and quickly solved, with students returning to classes ready to learn the disciplinary content (Stevenson & Kokkinn 2009; Wingate 2006).

The view of ELP as foundational to disciplinary learning in effect separates ELP from disciplinary teaching and learning. This positioning of the role of ELP to disciplinary learning means that disciplinary academics do not consider it their responsibility to address ELP within their teaching, learning and assessment tasks.

47

As a result little, if any, collaboration is required between English language specialists and disciplinary academics.

Status of academic language and learning staff

As we have argued, situating academic language and learning practices on the margins of academic life may create difficulties for English language specialists in collaborating with disciplinary academics. It is not necessarily the location of the support unit or centre that is the problem, as staff from decentralised support services can also find it difficult to develop collaborative practices (Peach 2003) with academics. Part of the problem is that responsibility for English language proficiency falls on English language specialists and not on the disciplinary academics. Yet it can be difficult for ALL staff to find opportunities to talk to disciplinary academics as the structures within institutions do not necessarily support collaboration. Typically, those who are ALL advisers have heavier teaching loads than disciplinary academics, which leaves them little time for interaction with disciplinary colleagues (Chanock 2007b). In addition, Chanock points out that there are fewer senior positions and many ALL advisers clustering at the lower levels of the academic ladder, who appear to have limited gravitas when it comes to discussing teaching, learning and assessment practices with disciplinary academics, largely because of their academic standing within the institution.

A related issue is the qualification levels of ALL staff involved in supporting students with English as an additional language. Arkoudis and Starfield (2007) randomly selected 10 institutions' ALL websites where they sought to find information about the English language qualifications of the staff. They found that only one website clearly indicated that all lecturers had postgraduate qualifications in applied linguistics and/or teaching English as a second or foreign language. Three ALL units ranged from about 30 to 60 per cent with similar qualifications. It was difficult to find the qualifications of the staff in the remaining six websites. Arkoudis and Starfield argued that

> The information gained from this exercise is inconclusive about the number of ALL staff with English language teaching qualifications. It does raise the question about what skills are

necessary for ALL staff. Should they require a Teaching English to Speakers of Other Language (TESOL) qualification? Do they need to know about the cultures of disciplinary teaching? Should they have a PhD if they are offering advice to PhD students? To what extent do they need to balance their knowledge of language and disciplinary teaching? Clearly, they need to be skilled professionals with postgraduate qualifications and a sophisticated skill set who can confidently engage with colleagues in disciplinary fields (p. 25).

Yet others argue that it is necessary for academic language and learning staff to have some background in the academic discipline if they are to have any epistemological authority in collaborating with disciplinary staff (Bruce 2008). It is not clear what the disciplinary background should be for those involved in addressing the language development of students with English as an additional language.

Evaluating the effectiveness of English language programs

It is difficult to evaluate the effectiveness of English language programs. The main reason for this is that there are a number of factors that influence English language development. To control these variables in order to evaluate the influence of English language programs on students' language development can be difficult. One of the most common approaches to evaluating programs is conducting pre- and post-test to measure the influence of the English language program on student improvement. There are two main difficulties with this approach. The first is that if the period between the pre- and post-tests is short (less than six months), then the post-test may not indicate any improvement because English language development does not occur overnight. Rather, it is complex and needs to be measured over a long period of time. Second, in pre- and post-tests, it is difficult to control the other variables that may influence English language development, such as employment, socialising with English speakers or living with English speakers. As was discussed in the introductory chapter, these factors can profoundly influence an individual's

English language ability. Any evaluation will need to include background data about the students that may inform the results received in the post-test. Findings would also be strengthened if the interviews were conducted with students to understand the factors that influence their English language development.

In an attempt to compare EAL international students' performance with other groups of students many higher education institutions analyse the academic progress of different student cohorts. This tracking activity can assist in identifying whether international students are performing at similar levels to local students. This information is useful for an institution, as underperformance of international students can subsequently be addressed. However, it is difficult for institutions' student systems to document the number of English language programs that students attend, particularly if they are one-to-one consultation or workshops. Therefore, the academic progress of different cohorts of students will not be useful for evaluating the effectiveness of English language programs unless they are the credit-bearing subjects in English for academic purposes in which students formally enrol.

Post-enrolment language assessment, otherwise known as English language diagnostic assessment, is increasingly being used by Australian institutions as a means of identifying the English language proficiency needs of students entering higher education (Dunworth 2009; Murray 2010). Early diagnosis of students' needs means that these are identified early in their course of study and can be addressed. There are different types of post-enrolment language assessments used in Australian institutions. In some institutions, institution-wide diagnostic tests are employed to identify students with particular needs and to direct them towards English language support programs. In other institutions, faculty and department-based assessments are used to assess the preparedness of students for higher education. The Measuring the Academic Skills of University Students diagnostic procedure, for example, involves tasks that are developed by disciplinary academic and academic language and learning staff. On completion of these tasks, students are given feedback on their strengths and weaknesses and are advised on what measures to take to further develop their writing (Arkoudis & Starfield 2007).

While the introduction of institution-wide diagnostic testing has increased awareness of English language proficiency in higher education institutions, it also raises significant challenges. It is difficult to ensure that students take the test and attend the recommended English language programs (Ransom 2009). This can result in resources being placed into administering post-enrolment language assessments for very little additional benefit. Most post-enrolment language assessments do not test speaking, which is a distinct disadvantage, particularly since spoken communication skills greatly influence the employment prospects of EAL students (Arkoudis et al. 2009). Given that we know that EAL students will encounter some difficulties in developing their English language in higher education, perhaps resources for institution-wide post-enrolment language assessments could be better used in resourcing English language offerings within institutions.

A final point that needs to be considered is the issue of learning transfer, which refers to the extent to which students transfer their learning from English language programs to mainstream classes. M. James (2010) has conducted research that has found that aspects of the mainstream teaching and learning context negatively influenced students' learning transfer. These aspects included instructors'/peers' explicit negative references to English for Academic Purposes (EAP) courses; instructors'/peers' ineffective or careless language use; and little or no connection between language use and grades' (p. 133).

The above discussion has highlighted the diverse activities available in higher education institutions to support students with English as an additional language. Some of these, such as establishing the success of their programs and integrating English language proficiency within disciplinary learning, should be high on the agenda of activities, given the emphasis on teaching and learning standards in Australian higher education (see Chapter 4). Other activities, such as professional development, can be effectively addressed through information resources, an example of which is presented below.

Practical strategies to enhance students' learning

Research has found that academics are aware of their students' learning needs, but may be unclear about how best to address those

needs. The purpose of this guide is to encourage the use of different strategies and approaches that have been informed by research. The key areas that are discussed in some detail include
- making lectures accessible
- encouraging participation in small group work
- adopting an educative approach to plagiarism
- supporting students in developing critical thinking skills
- explaining assessment expectations.

The practical advice in this section has been written for academic staff who wish to explore different ideas in their teaching to address the needs of international students with English as an additional language. It includes reflections and advice from Australian academic teaching staff (with each quote referenced to indicate the broad field of education in which they are teaching). This advice, which has been adapted from Arkoudis (2006), is offered with EAL students in mind but can be useful for all students.

Making lectures accessible

Understanding lecture content can be difficult for EAL students. Listening, an active rather than a passive skill, requires EAL students to process the words, attempt to understand the main ideas presented and draw on what they already know to make sense of the material presented in the lecture, in what may be their second, third or fourth language. This is especially true for first year undergraduate and postgraduate EAL students, who are in the early stages of developing their English language skills in an academic context and may also be adapting to culturally unfamiliar approaches to learning. Despite these challenges, there are a number of strategies that can be used in the design and delivery of the lecture that can assist in making the conventional lecture more accessible for international students.
- Outline the main points of the lecture and make links to other topics covered in the subject or material to be covered in tutorials. Highlight key questions or issues that will be addressed during the lecture. Concept maps are useful as they offer a visual representation of the content and how it relates to other areas in the course.

- Provide a lecture outline with the main points to be covered to assist students to follow the lecture and guide their notetaking. These can be put on the web for students to download and supplement the PowerPoint slides that are usually available to students.
- Explain any relevant background information that may assist students in understanding key concepts.
- Include a glossary.
- Define any new or unfamiliar words or concepts, and provide opportunities for clarification.
- If slang, jargon and culturally specific humour are used in the lecture, explain the meaning for students who may not understand them. This is particularly important for first year students.
- Summarise the important information at different stages in the lecture.
- Record the lecture, so that international students can listen to it again. This will assist students to clarify points that they may have not understood due to English being their second or third language.
- Conclude the lecture by summarising the main points and highlighting take home messages. The following statement by an academic is an example of how you might go about this.

> In my lectures I think critically about the level of detail I teach. I think about what is more important. Is there a theoretical concept or an overview that the students would much rather have than being bogged down with the seventy-seven new words that we are introducing in today's lecture?
>
> Academic, Chemistry

Creating opportunities for small group participation

It has been widely observed that EAL students may appear hesitant to contribute to group discussions. This is not necessarily because this is their preferred learning style; EAL students often report that they would like to participate but lack the confidence to do so. One reason for the lack of confidence could be in part due to their lack of familiarity with how to contribute to an academic discussion or their perceived lack of English language skills. Contributing to discussions can be seen as a risky undertaking if students are not comfortable with their English language ability or are unfamiliar with the cultural conventions governing breaking in to the conversation. Academics may need to create safe learning environments in which students feel that they can make a contribution. Creating opportunities for participation in class so students feel supported can be achieved by incorporating some of the following strategies.

Preparation for small group discussion

- EAL students need to be given adequate time to prepare responses. One strategy that can be used is to ask students to prepare some responses for the next tutorial or seminar. Set key questions with the reading material so that students can prepare their answer before the class. Preparation will give them greater confidence in contributing to any discussion.
- It is important to make your expectations about students' participation clear to them. As we know, this is an effective strategy for all students, but it is particularly useful for international students because research indicates that they are often not aware of what participation in class actually means in an Australian tertiary context. Making academic expectations clear can help to clarify this to students.
- Early in the semester create a teaching atmosphere in which students interact with each other. This provides students from different backgrounds with the opportunity to talk and get to know each other.

> I spend a lot of time in the first class breaking the ice and getting the students to establish a bond and start making friendships. By the end of the class I can hardly stop them from talking. And I do this in my lectures as well as small group teaching.
>
> Academic, Arts

Encouraging contributions in class

One way of increasing participation is to memorise students' names and invite them to speak. If the lecturer has already established a

safe environment and if students feel that the group values their contributions this can be a successful strategy. Other valuable strategies include the following.
- Ask students how the issue would be considered from their experiences, keeping in mind that they do not represent the views of their culture or country.
- Pose questions or issues that students can discuss in pairs and then report back to the class.
- Remember to wait before moving on to another student; it can take time for EAL students to understand the question, consider their response and communicate that in English.
- Structure group tasks so that EAL and non-EAL students are grouped together. Assign roles for each member of the small group, including discussion leader, timekeeper, notetaker and a person to report back. This enables everyone to have a role in the group.
- Activities such as quizzes and pair work are valuable in encouraging interaction among students.
- Organising group activities so that diversity of experience and knowledge are necessary for successfully completing the task.

Adopting an educative approach to plagiarism

Cultural and language issues can lead to misunderstandings about plagiarism for EAL students. Students need to know what constitutes plagiarism (see *Assessing Learning In Australian Universities*, www.cshe.unimelb.edu.au/assessinglearning). For EAL students, plagiarism can be an intercultural issue. They may come from cultures in which writing involves repeating the collective wisdom and there is little need to acknowledge the source of information. Plagiarism can also be an English language ability issue. While EAL students may be aware of what plagiarism is, they may lack the English language skills required to read information, extract the relevant points, and then put it into their own words to avoid plagiarising.
- Highlight the reasons why referencing is used in your discipline and give students examples of correct referencing styles.

> When the students begin their first assignment I spend some time in class explaining how to use referencing. I highlight how they should include references in their notes and where they got that

information. I give the students a style guide to help them and ask them to refer to it all the time when they are writing.

Academic, History

- Model the use of referencing in your lectures and tutorials.
- In the discussion of readings, highlight sections where the author has synthesised the main ideas and referenced them.
- Use examples of previous assignments to demonstrate how ideas can be presented and sources referenced.
- Develop tasks that ask students to evaluate and analyse ideas they have read, so that the focus is more on critiquing the readings rather than comprehension.

Rather than focus on what the students should not do in terms of plagiarism, I try to focus on what the students should be doing. I want the students to synthesise and evaluate what they read. We need to teach students how to do this and this needs to be more of a focus in teaching.

Academic, Management

Supporting students to develop critical thinking skills

It is often suggested that students from Confucian heritage cultures find it difficult to think critically. As is the case with most stereotypes, this is unlikely to be true. Research has found that students from Confucian heritage cultures are capable of high-level critical thinking. It is not the students' cognitive skills that are in question, it is their English language ability that influences their reading, understanding, interpretation and evaluation of the material that is demonstrated in written or oral expression. As we know, developing critical thinking skills is equally challenging for students from backgrounds other than Confucian heritage cultures.

There are a number of possible strategies for teaching critical thinking skills. Classroom activities that model critical thinking skills in discussions, create learning opportunities for students to develop their skills and offer feedback can guide students' development of critical thinking skills. These may include the following.

Models of English language programs

- Explain and demonstrate what critical thinking skills are required in your disciplinary area. Different disciplines define critical thinking in slightly different ways.
- Highlight the importance of the reading material to the content of the course. This will assist students to access the main ideas presented in the texts and will guide them in prioritising their reading, something that is particularly useful for EAL students.
- When setting required readings, offer students questions to guide their reading of the text. Stage the questions to include literal meaning (describe, define, explain), interpretive meaning (analyse, test, calculate, apply, demonstrate) and applied meaning (evaluate, compare, assess). This will help the students to think beyond the literal understanding and develop their skills as strategic and critical readers.
- Develop students' critical thinking skills through classroom discussions. Questions such as 'In what situations would this work?', 'Can you think of any situation in which this would not apply?' and 'How does this relate to other theories or concepts we have discussed?' can be used as prompts for students to present different points of view.

Explaining assessment expectations

Assessment may be one of the most important areas in which students need to be given guidance. As students bring a range of educational experiences to higher education, it is useful to highlight what will be valued in the assessment process, which requires explaining the assessment criteria and expectations as well as offering constructive feedback to students (for more information see *Guide for Reviewing Assessment*, www.cshe.unimelb.edu.au/publications). Feedback is especially important to EAL students as it can offer them some direction on how they can improve their written English language skills.

Assessment criteria

- Explain in detail the purpose of the assessment and the subject content being assessed. Give students a copy of the assessment criteria and explain how marks will be allocated, which gives students a clearer understanding of what is required and clarifies expectations.

[English Language Standards in Higher Education

- Indicate in the criteria which aspects of English language will be assessed and the marks allocated for it.
- Outline the requirements of any exam and model the type of responses required.

> Two weeks before the exam, I run cases and sample questions similar to the exam and I clearly explain to them what they will get points for in answering the question and how they should answer it. I focus on the structure as well as the content. For instance, if I'm going to give any marks for definition, I will always say to the students that they need to give a definition. I emphasise that they need to have an introduction, body and conclusion and that I will give so many points for each part.
>
> Academic, Economics

Assessment and learning

- To cater for different learning styles try, where possible, to vary the type of assessment tasks used.

> I try to provide a range of assessment tasks, so I will have a combination of group assessment, of individual assessment and multiple choices. I'll also have participation in class as part of the formal assessment and the exam.
>
> Academic, Science

- Assessment tasks early in the semester can help to identify students who may need extra support with their English writing.
- Plan learning activities that prepare the students for the assessment tasks. This is useful for all students and increases understanding of the requirements of the assessment for the subject. It also allows opportunities for group feedback.

Feedback

- Try to avoid feedback such as 'This is not logical' or 'This is confusing', as these comments do not offer students advice on how they can improve. If the paper does not flow logically, then offer a few brief suggestions to the students as to how

they achieve this and direct them to English language services available at the institution.
- Offer oral feedback to students in class after assignments have been returned. Focus on the main issues that arose from the assessment and identify what students can do to improve their performance in subsequent assessments for the subject.

Strategies to enhance development programs

Below are a few suggestions that can shift the focus of English language programs from support to development. These suggestions focus on developing a program that is evaluated in terms of addressing the English language development needs of EAL students. Such a program can be used to develop evidence-based arguments for the continued resourcing of the program.
- Use English language development rather than support.
- Develop institutional plans to monitor and evaluate students' English language development.
- Develop a strategic plan for English language programs that identifies program options and how they will be evaluated.
- Develop priorities for research and publish findings.
- Employ at least a few academic staff who will be able to undertake research to identify areas for further program improvement.
- Use second language acquisition research as the basis for informing teaching and learning practices in English language programs.

Summary

One of the main challenges of English language support programs is that they have their origins in working with students who are at risk of failing due to their lack of English language proficiency. English language difficulties are viewed as a deficit, so any assistance is seen to be remedial. English language support is positioned as institutionally separate from disciplinary teaching. Even though there has been a slight shift as English language support units seek to work with disciplinary academics to support EAL students with English language, the focus of these programs is on English language support, rather than development.

The *Good Practice Principles*, which outlines a set of general statements for Australian higher education institutions to address in the context of their own operations and environment, emphasises the importance of a variety of activities that are integrated across the curriculum (Australian Universities Quality Agency 2009, p. 10):

> while there is no single 'best' way to develop students' English language proficiency, contextualisation within the disciplines and integration of language development across the curriculum seem likely to be effective approaches. 'Integration' in this context means taking a holistic view across a discipline to address needs across a variety of means, including: embedding language development through curriculum design and assessment; workshops or credit-bearing units within a course; 'adjunct' workshops or sessions within a course; developing workplace communication through preparation for work placements and practica; and targeted individual or group support provided by academic language and learning experts.

While a variety of programs can exist, they need to be linked to teaching and learning within the discipline and result in developing a holistic view of ELP across a discipline. In addition, higher education institutions are required to 'use evidence from a variety of sources to monitor and improve their English language development activities' (AUQA 2010, p. 14). What this means is that having a variety of English language programs is not in itself sufficient to ensure ELP standards in higher education. In addition to these practices, institutions are required to gather evidence that monitors and improves the various ELP activities. Recent reports (AUQA 2010) have highlighted this, with particular comments from audit panels recommending that institutions consider indicators and evidence in order to establish the success of their ELP programs, as well as developing approaches to integrate ELP within disciplinary teaching. Unless English language is incorporated within curriculum planning, it fails to feature where it matters most – within disciplinary teaching and learning. The next chapter will explore this in more detail.

CHAPTER 4

INTEGRATING ENGLISH LANGUAGE LEARNING IN THE DISCIPLINES

It makes sense for English language development to be linked to disciplinary teaching and learning. Language is not a content-free medium. Transmission methods of teaching and learning may view language as simply a conduit to teaching the content of the subject, where knowledge and content are transmitted to the student. Yet research has repeatedly found that language is an important means by which students participate, understand and develop the academic discourse of their discipline. Studies have also shown that academic discourse varies across disciplines. Having discussed various models of English language support in higher education in the previous chapter, this chapter focuses on the arguments for adopting a discipline-based approach to English language development in higher education. Through examination of a case study that involves the development of a content-based English language program in the discipline of architecture, some of the conditions that can support or hinder these programs in higher education institutions are investigated. From the lessons learnt in the case study, we discuss the requirements necessary for integrating English language programs in the disciplines.

Generic or specific? An ongoing debate

For a number of decades, language experts have debated whether English language programs should focus on general or (discipline-) specific language work. In the 1980s, prominent scholars (for example, Hutchinson & Waters 1987; Spack 1988; Widdowson 1983) argued for a wide angle or generic approach to language provision with a focus on the language and skills common to all disciplines. These scholars argued that there are features of English common to all areas and that the focus should be on teaching generic forms and skills that are transferable across disciplines (Hyland 2002). Hutchinson and Waters (1987) argued that because there are not enough differences in the discourse structure and grammar of different disciplines, there is little justification for subject-specific approaches to English language teaching. In her much quoted article, Spack (1988) also questioned English language specialists' expertise and ability to teach subject-specific conventions. She argued that language specialists should focus their energies on teaching general English principles and rhetoric, and leave the subject-specific teaching to the subject specialists.

Until the 1990s, most programs in English for academic purposes offered in UK and Australian higher education institutions were of the generic kind. In the 2000s, however, there has been a shift in the types of English programs offered in institutions. Although general programs in English for academic purposes continue to dominate, there is a growing belief among language specialists that students need more embedded, discipline-specific approaches to English language development that involves concurrent teaching of language and disciplinary content (Baik & Greig 2009). One of the main concerns raised about generic language programs is that they are extracurricular, that is, they lie outside the mainstream curricula and courses that students undertake. Students are, then, unlikely to recognise the relevance of these generic courses to their subjects (Wingate 2006); consequently, attendance in these programs is typically low. Durkin and Main (2002), who report on programs in the UK, note that students most in need of support and further development do not attend these programs. Rather, these extracurricular programs more often attract high-achieving students who are already performing at a high level, a common experience also reported by those working in Australian institutions (Baik & Greig 2009).

More importantly, aside from the issue of attendance, researchers have asserted that generic programs alone are not sufficient for the high-level study necessary for students with

English as an additional language to perform effectively in their disciplines (Bruce 2002; Hyland 2002; Peelo & Luxon 2007). Most undergraduate courses require students to demonstrate expertise in a variety of written genres. To succeed in their courses, students need to learn that there are certain ways of writing and forms of expression that signify membership in the relevant disciplinary discourse community. Dudley-Evans and St John (1998) explain that although all academic disciplines share a common core of language and discoursal features, text analyses from various disciplines show significant differences at the genre level. Mackiewicz's study (2004), for example, shows that the written genres in engineering disciplines are considerably different to genres required of students in other disciplines. She stresses the importance of providing advice on writing in a discipline-specific context. This supports the argument that fundamental differences in the genre and academic conventions of disciplines necessitate a discipline-specific approach to institutions' language development programs (Hyland 2000, 2003; North 2005). In other words, English language work should be embedded in specific disciplines.

The argument for discipline-specific approaches

Different disciplines require different types of knowledge and competencies and the work on disciplinary differences is plentiful. Neumann's (2001, p. 144) research shows that these differences have a strong influence on 'academics' beliefs, on teaching and on students' learning'. In their influential work on academic cultures, Becher and Trowler (2001, p. 41) note that by analysing disciplinary discourse, one can 'discern differences in the modes in which arguments are generated, developed, expressed and reported'. We know, for example, that the reading and writing tasks required of students are specific to discipline and 'every specific discipline has its own conventions, values and practices' (Durkin & Main 2002, p. 26). Hyland (2000) thus argues that the academic practices of reading and writing should not be seen as 'general skills', but rather as the 'core of each discipline'. Geertz (1983, p. 155, cited in Hyland 2000, p. 145) describes disciplinary approaches as 'ways of being in the world'. North's study (2005) on arts and science essays, for instance, shows that there are social and epistemological differences between disciplines, that is, what constitutes legitimate knowledge and how it is presented. The essays of students with arts backgrounds presented knowledge as mediated and contested, while those with science backgrounds presented the object of a study as a representation of reality with less interpretation and evaluation. From an arts perspective, writing deals with interpretation, is complex and requires careful expression, while from a science perspective, writing deals with facts, is succinct and straightforward.

Hyland (2002, p. 390) explains that the principle of specificity is underpinned by a social constructionist view, that is, members of a discipline or profession jointly create and sustain their particular view of the world through their distinctive discourses. As Elbow states, 'in using a discourse we are also tacitly teaching a version of reality and the student's place and mode of operation in it' (1991, p. 146). For students to succeed in their courses and later in their professions, they need to develop an understanding of, and proficiency in, the distinctive discourses of their discipline.

Another theoretical perspective that lends support to the principle of specificity is offered by Lave and Wenger's (1991) theory of legitimate peripheral participation. These authors explain that the aim of learning is to move from peripheral to full participation in communities of practice, a process, they argue, that necessarily must occur within a discipline. This concept of learning as participation involves the construction of identities grounded within a disciplinary community. As communicative events are socially situated within discourse communities that have an agreed structure and purpose (Swales 1990), potential members must learn the structures and conventions to become accepted into these communities in which they are based. Dressen-Hammouda (2008) argues that student learning is best done within the discipline in which they are developing a disciplinary identity, which means embedding the language learning in the discipline – in other words, including English language development in the teaching and learning of disciplinary content.

The numerous cognitive and linguistic benefits of disciplinary content-based English language programs have been demonstrated in a number of studies (for example, Kasper 1997; Kennelly,

Integrating English language learning in the disciplines

Maldoni, & Davis 2010; Song 2006; Winter 2000). In addition to increased interest and motivation, these programs have been shown to lead to positive academic outcomes. In his study of the effects of content-based study on students' future academic performance, for example, Song (2006, p. 421) shows that students who received content-based language instruction achieved 'comparable or even better mastery of disciplinary content' than students who did not receive content-based language instruction. He concludes that content-based English language programs 'promote both language acquisition and academic success'. As Stoller (2002, p. 3) aptly puts it: 'When we promote the acquisition of [disciplinary] content, simultaneously we're going to be helping our students master language.'

The following section presents a case study of a program designed by language specialists at the University of Melbourne in Australia to embed English language development into the disciplinary learning of students with English as an additional language undertaking a core architectural history subject. While the focus of the case study is on the discipline of architecture, it provides insights into some of the issues and challenges that emerge for English language specialists as they attempt to integrate English language proficiency with disciplinary learning and how these might be addressed, and is thus relevant to all other disciplines.

Importantly, the case study reports on attempts to monitor and evaluate students' ELP learning. The ideas discussed in the case study can inform programs across disciplines and contexts as it is not the disciplinary context that is important, rather, it is the tasks involved in integrating ELP into an established educational discipline. In integrating ELP into the disciplines, the English language specialists' aim is to bring English language development into the core curriculum of a course of study and thereby eliminate the 'artificial separation between language and content courses' (Song 2006, p. 422). As Hyland (2002, p. 390) asserts:

> The teaching of specific skills and rhetoric cannot be divorced from the teaching of a subject itself because what counts as convincing argument, appropriate tone, persuasive interaction, and so on, is managed for a particular audience.

CASE STUDY: INTEGRATING ENGLISH LANGUAGE AND DISCIPLINARY LEARNING

At The University of Melbourne, international students make up more than 25 per cent of the total student population, and there are increasing numbers of domestic students from backgrounds with English as an additional language. The proportion of EAL students in the Faculty of Architecture, Building and Planning in 2006 was well over 40 per cent and likely to grow. For a number of years there had been growing concern among academic staff in the faculty that EAL students were struggling to cope with the demands of their courses. Inadequate English language proficiency was seen as one of the main reasons for the high number of unsatisfactory results among students, particularly in theoretical and linguistically demanding subjects. There was general agreement that EAL students needed to be more effectively supported to develop necessary language and academic skills so they could satisfactorily complete their course. It is in this context that the faculty sought advice from language specialists in the university's central Academic Skills Unit about the best way to support the English language development of their EAL students.

Analysing students' language learning needs

The first step in developing a program in English for academic purposes for architecture students was to conduct a needs analysis to look at the target needs of the students in the architectural history subject as well as those in the whole architecture course. The outcome would inform the instructional priorities.

The language specialists sought to embed a semester-long tutorial program in one of the core first year subjects. Architectural courses typically involve students having to complete theoretical subjects in their first year. These subjects, which are designed to give a historical context to architecture, require students to produce extended written assignments, often in the form of an academic research essay. The linguistic demands of these subjects are challenging for all first year undergraduate students, particularly for EAL students.

The needs analysis included numerous discussions with the subject lecturers as well as one of the subject specialist tutors. From these early meetings, the language specialists assessed student learning priorities from the perspectives of the subject specialists and collected examples of key texts commonly used in the study of architecture and architectural history. In addition, the language specialists had several discussions with later year EAL students undertaking the architecture course to obtain their perspective on the learning needs and challenges of EAL students in the course. Based on their experience with EAL students in the course, the academic teaching staff, who were frustrated by student work when meaning was obscured by numerous grammatical and semantic errors, raised four issues or priorities:

- Understanding of the topics through clear (and accurate) written expression must be demonstrated in the following ways.
- Writing must be in a style appropriate for the discipline.
- Architectural source texts must be used appropriately in writing.
- Contribution to tutorial discussions and activities must be active.

From the perspective of later year students, the first year architectural history subject was considered to be extremely demanding. Three issues were particularly emphasised by students:

- understanding the large volume of content covered in weekly lectures and readings, and applying this to written assignments
- learning to appropriately use the discipline's vocabulary
- completing all the components of the final written exam.

Text analysis

In addition to the discussion with staff and students, the needs analysis process involved analysis of the language features – genres and discourse – of a range of texts commonly used in the study of architecture and architectural history as well as the types of texts students would be required to produce (Dudley-Evans & St John 1998; Hyland 2003). This involved examination of assessment tasks, assessment criteria and written examinations that students would have to complete in the course of their studies, not just in the first-year architectural history subject, but in the course overall. The analysis revealed that the most common functions architecture students are required to perform are to:

- identify and describe characteristics and features of particular architectural styles
- describe and compare different styles or approaches
- describe and evaluate (critique and defend) designs and approaches.

Description is an important genre within the discipline of architecture, which means that the ability to produce an articulate description is an essential skill an architect needs to have, whether it is to explain styles, identify precedents, consider influences or present one's design. Berkenkotter and Huckin (1995, p. 3) assert that knowledge of genre is 'a form of situated cognition embedded in disciplinary activities'. By focusing on the function of description in the tutorial program, the aim was to help students develop 'transferable' disciplinary language skills necessary for other or future subjects in their architecture course.

Diagnostic assessment task
All students enrolled in the first year architecture program were asked to complete a diagnostic written exercise during the first lecture of a core European architecture subject. The aim of the task was to assess students' written skills and identify those students who had poor writing skills. Although it was argued that all first year students would benefit from an increased focus on the development of English language skills, resource constraints meant that a small program targeting students most in need of support had to be developed.

For the writing exercise, students were asked to identify and describe a public building (anywhere in the world) and explain why it was significant to them. This exercise reflects the kinds of descriptive writing tasks architecture students regularly undertake.

Students' writing was assessed by the language specialists using an analytical marking guide that included discourse-level features such as logical organisation, paragraph structure, coherence and cohesion, and word- and sentence-level features such as vocabulary use, syntax and grammar. All students received feedback on their writing in the form of a completed marking sheet indicating writing strengths and weaknesses.

Of the 186 students enrolled in the architectural history subject, 37 students (19.9 per cent) were identified as needing 'substantial improvement' and were enrolled in the adjunct tutorials in English as a second language. All 37 students were from EAL backgrounds and most were international students from South-East Asian countries. It was apparent that many EAL students perceived these tutorials to be potentially beneficial to their learning. Students who had not been enrolled in the classes requested permission to attend; the attendance rate was consistently high throughout the semester.

Course design and structure
The tutorial program in EAP for architecture students was based on the US 'adjunct' model (Snow & Brinton 1988) in which there is concurrent teaching of two courses: architectural history taught by the content lecturer and the EAP tutorial program taught by language specialists. Within an overall content-based pedagogical approach, the EAP tutorial course was structured around the 'real world' academic tasks that students would have to perform

Integrating English language learning in the disciplines

(Stoller 2002). For the students in European architecture this case meant small-group presentations, a research essay and a timed written examination for which students would be expected to produce extended responses to essay-type questions.

The adjunct EAP tutorial program consisted of weekly 90-minute group tutorials with approximately 18 students assigned to each tutorial. The EAP tutorials were scheduled to take place after the weekly lecture and before the regular subject tutorials. The timetabling of the EAP tutorials was important. Each tutorial was based on the content introduced in the weekly lectures and the set readings, and every tutorial session included learning activities designed to help students consolidate and articulate their understanding of core concepts in the subject. The objective in scheduling the EAP tutorials to take place before the regular subject tutorials was to give students with English as an additional language opportunities to practise discussion skills based on the concepts, designs and buildings introduced in the week's lectures. It was hoped that this would enable them to be more confident contributors to the main tutorial. Discussion with disciplinary tutors suggested that there had been some improvement in this area.

To ensure that the tutorials were firmly grounded in the content of the subject, the language specialists attended all the lectures and content tutorials, and communicated frequently with academic teaching staff. This collaboration with disciplinary academic staff was essential for the language specialists to find out about the conceptual and discoursal framework of the subject (Dudley-Evans & St John 1998). It would not have been possible for the language specialists to develop a discipline-specific program integrating language and subject content without ongoing collaboration with the disciplinary academics.

The tutorials were designed to build students' knowledge and skills to complete the common assessment tasks for the subject (and overall course of study). In particular, teaching and learning activities focused on enabling students to use the language of architecture to describe buildings and designs introduced in the subject. There were several reasons for the language specialists' decision to focus on the major assessment tasks. The first was related to student motivation and engagement. Clearly, student learning is greatly influenced by assessment (see, for example, Biggs & Tang 2007; Dunworth 2008; Maclellan 2004; Ramsden 2003). The language specialists believed that students would be motivated to participate actively in the adjunct tutorial program only if the learning was related to summative assessment in the subject. The English language tutorials had to be seen as equal in importance or of relevance to their regular subject tutorial.

In addition to this, the language specialists believed it was important to examine the assessment tasks, because doing so would enable them to signal to students 'the kind of intellectual work which is valued' in their discipline (Maclellan 2004, p. 20). Analysing the assessment tasks would then provide the students with some insight into the 'underlying value system and epistemological position' of the discipline of architecture (Dunworth 2008, p. 321). Doing this would enable them to move closer, from 'peripheral' to 'full participation' in the architecture community of practice (Lave & Wenger 1991).

Program evaluation

Evaluation of the program consisted of mid and end of course student surveys to explore students' perceptions of the program and analyses of students' academic performance. The researchers (Baik & Greig 2009) were concerned with whether students who participated in the program achieved better results for the subject than students who did not. They also wanted to know whether the knowledge, skills and strategies developed in the program were transferred to their learning in other subjects.

Student perceptions

From the students' perspective, the adjunct tutorial program was beneficial to their learning in the subject. Students were asked to indicate the extent to which they agreed with statements on a five point Likert scale. As indicated in Table 4.1, 100 per cent of students agreed or strongly agreed that the tutorials had been relevant and useful; the mean rating for the overall usefulness of the program was 4.5 out of a possible 5. A slightly lower proportion of students (68 per cent) believed that their language and academic skills had improved after participating in the program, which may be related not to

Table 4.1: Summary of student evaluations in English for academic purposes

		% agree or strongly agree	Average rating (out of 5)
1	The content of the tutorials has been relevant and useful	100	4.7
2	I feel my language and academic skills have improved	68	3.8
3	The teachers were effective	100	4.5
4	Overall, the tutorials have been helpful or useful	100	4.5

students' perceptions of the course, but to students' unrealistic expectations and beliefs about improving their language skills (Fegan 2006; Sawir 2002).

Academic performance

To examine the effectiveness of the adjunct tutorial program in English for academic purposes for architecture students, the English language specialists undertook an evaluation study immediately after the course and again 12 months later to assess the impact of the program on students' academic performance. A detailed account of the findings of this study is provided in Baik and Greig (2009). Overall, the findings suggest positive effects of the discipline-based writing program on students' overall academic outcomes.

The findings from the evaluation study summarised in Table 4.2 showed that the pass rate for students who frequently attended 80 per cent or more of the English as a second language tutorials was 100 per cent, and 91.7 per cent for those who attended 60 to 80 per cent of tutorials, whereas it was only 31.3 per cent for those who attended less than 60 per cent of tutorials. This was in contrast to a pass rate of 77.9 per cent for all other students in the subject. Similarly, the average mark obtained by students who frequently attended the English for academic purposes tutorials was 63.8 per cent, slightly above the average of 60.1 per cent for all other students in the subject, and considerably higher than the average mark for students who did not frequently attend the tutorials. The average mark for these students was 33.3 per cent, a mark well below the minimum level (50 per cent) required to pass the subject.

These findings are consistent with a study conducted by Winter (2000), who examined the academic outcomes of students with English as a second language in a content-linked psychology course. She found that in the final exam, the students with English as a second language who participated in the program performed significantly better with an average mark of 89.11 than the

Table 4.2: Pass rate and average mark for students in European architecture

	Pass rate (%)	Average mark (%)
Students in EAP tutorials		
Those who attended most frequently (n=9)	100.0	63.8
Moderate attendees (n=12)	91.7	58.4
Low attendees (n=16)	31.3	33.3
All other students (n=149)	77.9	60.1

Source: Baik & Grieg 2009, p. 411

mainstream group who obtained an average of 66.86 (p. 78). More recently, a study by Kennelly, Maldoni and Davis (2010) also showed positive learning outcomes for students who had participated in a discipline-specific program. Their study showed that, whereas 95 per cent of students with English as an additional language who had attended the content-based course in English for academic purposes passed the subject, most of those who did not attend failed. The authors also note that the discipline-specific programs had a positive effect on student retention at their institution (Kennelly et al. 2010).

To examine the longer-term effects of the EAP tutorial program, the academic results of students with English as an additional language enrolled in that program were tracked and analysed. The findings 12 months after the program show that the academic outcomes of students who regularly attended the EAP tutorial program were higher than those for students who failed to attend the program regularly. The retention rate was 100 per cent for frequent and moderate attendees and 84.2 per cent for low attendees. In the year following the program, frequent attendees achieved an average mark of 65.8 per cent for all their subjects, whereas for low attendees the average mark for all subjects undertaken was 51.8 per cent (Baik & Greig 2009). These findings support a larger-scale study conducted by Song (2006, p. 420), who compared the results of 385 students enrolled in a content-based program in English as a second language with 385 students who did not receive content-based instruction. He found that students who participated in the content-linked program had 'better long-term academic success rates' than the students who did not participate in the content-based language program.

It is evident that the approach to embedding language development in disciplinary learning described in this case study contributed to positive academic outcomes for students who participated in the English language tutorial program. While we acknowledge that there could be a number of factors – academic, social, personal – that influenced the outcomes for the students in the architecture English language tutorial program, Baik and Greig's (2009) findings support previous studies on content-based EAP programs (Kasper 1997; Skillen 2006; Song 2006). We argue, after Song (2006, p. 434), that integrating language learning with disciplinary content learning can assist students with English as an additional language 'accelerate academic English skills development, enhancing academic performance, and facilitate academic success'. Based on the case study presented here as well as the literature on curriculum development for English for academic purposes, the following section describes the conditions necessary for successfully integrating an English language program in the disciplines.

Integrating English language programs in the disciplines

There are five important conditions required to integrate English language programs into the disciplines. They are as follows.

A thorough needs analysis process

The important role of needs analysis in curriculum development for English for academic purposes has been well established and there is plentiful literature on needs analysis in the context of course design for English as a second language (Bacha & Bahous 2008; Jordan 1997; Long 2005; Taillefer 2007). In carrying out a thorough needs analysis, it is important to consider a number of factors including the following.

- *Target situation* – What activities or tasks do students need to be able to complete or perform? What language skills are needed for students to complete these tasks successfully?
- *The students* – What do students expect or want from the course? What has been their past experience with English language learning? What level or standard are their current English language skills? What are the gaps or weaknesses in their English language proficiency, that is, what areas are most in need of improvement?
- *The environment* – What are the available resources? What are the constraints, for example, time, classroom setting, class size?

Support of department leaders and disciplinary academics

There are many stories of language specialists who have tried to develop integrated discipline-specific programs for faculties, without success because of lack of support from departments. O'Loughlin and Arkoudis' study (2009) of language specialists and disciplinary staff perspectives on business and economics students' English language development highlights the value of support from faculty disciplinary staff in emphasising the importance of language development to students. As one language specialist notes:

> If English language development is strongly encouraged by the head of department, I think there would be a bigger take-up of the undergraduate program by academics than there currently is. It's really left up to the students to find out on their own, no one strongly encourages them from people who they see as being the leaders in the disciplinary teaching.
>
> O'Loughlin & Arkoudis 2009, p. 128

O'Loughlin and Arkoudis' study shows that without institutional support, it can be very difficult for language specialists to work with disciplinary staff. Leadership support can assist in recognising that responsibility for English language proficiency development rests with all teaching academics. Encouragement from department leaders and other staff could also help to raise awareness among students about the need to improve their English language while completing their degree. It appears that some students do not believe English language proficiency to be an important part of their studies. As one language specialist in O'Loughlin and Arkoudis' study reports: 'A lot of students have said to me, "But why are we worrying about language? We are doing a commerce degree. Why does anybody care about what our language is like?"'

Comments such as this raise questions about the expectations students have of their higher education and the role and importance of English language proficiency. Improvement in students' English language proficiency will only be made through concerted effort and work on the part of students. The role of department leaders and disciplinary teaching staff in managing student expectations and raising awareness about the importance of ongoing English language development is essential.

Highly qualified and flexible English language specialists

Support of disciplinary staff and department leaders is an important aspect in ensuring that students engage with English language programs. English language specialists play a crucial role in gaining the support of disciplinary staff. In the case study described above, the language experts developed a detailed and evidence-based proposal for the adjunct tutorial program in English for academic

purposes that was well-received and subsequently endorsed by the head of the architecture program. The key factors in the success of the proposal included the following.
- Arguments and suggestions were made with a strong evidence base from current research and literature in the field.
- The proposal was made with the faculty context and constraints – financial, space, timetabling – in mind; in other words, the language specialists demonstrated that they were aware of the local context of the faculty and were proposing reasonable suggestions.
- The intended learning outcomes or learning objectives of the program were clearly listed; in other words, the language specialists answered the key questions: Why should the faculty support this program? How will it assist students and staff in the faculty?

In developing an English language program such as the one described in this chapter, there are challenges for the language specialists who are working outside their discipline. As Bruce (2002, p. 340) reflects, 'the balance between language and content in such a course is a delicate one'. It requires well-qualified and knowledgeable language specialists who not only can draw on current research in English language teaching literature, but can also communicate effectively with disciplinary staff. Indeed, without the communication and interpersonal skills to collaborate well with disciplinary staff, attempts to integrate English language programs in the disciplines is likely to be ineffective.

English language specialists also need to be flexible in their approach and methods for delivering integrated language programs. They need to design programs with the specific context – needs, resources, structure – of the particular faculty in mind.

Continuous collaboration with discipline content specialists

The case of the adjunct tutorial in English for academic purposes in the Faculty of Architecture, Building and Planning described in the case study above shows the importance of collaborations. Without the input of the subject specialists, the language specialists would not have been able to design a tutorial program that integrated language learning and subject content. It is not possible for language specialists to have expertise in a number of disciplines. When developing courses for specific disciplines, language specialists will not, for the most part, have expertise in that subject area. It is essential, then, that language specialists work with academics who are developing and teaching the subjects in the discipline to design the EAP program and use the materials to develop appropriate activities that assist students to develop their English language proficiency and meet the intended learning outcomes of the disciplinary subject.

While there are those (for example, Spack 1988) who argue that language specialists should focus on general academic skills and rhetoric and leave the subject-specific conventions to the subject specialists themselves, we believe that, by working in collaboration with subject specialists, English language specialists are well positioned and qualified to bring a specific focus on to the language of the subject content. One of the objectives of the language specialists in this case study was to help students analyse and understand the ways language works to build meaning in their specific discipline. The aim was to help first year students build a strong foundation from which more complex language skills could be developed. Whether subject specialists would have the desire, let alone the expertise, to teach such skills is questionable. The model we argue for is one that involves close collaboration between language experts and discipline academics.

A major benefit of integrated programs in English for academic purposes, in addition to positive learning outcomes, can be the broader impact of the collaboration between the language specialists and the subject specialists. In the case study presented above, the collaboration between the language specialist and disciplinary expert worked to their mutual benefit: it enabled language specialists – who traditionally work in marginalised language and academic skills units on the periphery of mainstream courses – to contribute to faculty discussions of teaching and learning, specifically, in relation to the language learning needs of students with English as an additional language. These discussions enabled critical reflection on aspects of the core curriculum, particularly content coverage and assessment design. The collaboration also led to the content specialists reflecting on other aspects of their curriculum, particularly on the presentation of lecture and tutorial materials.

This early collaboration also planted the seeds for later ongoing collaborative work in the Faculty of Architecture, Building and Planning. Soon after the first adjunct tutorial program was completed, one of the language specialists in the case study was recruited as a staff member in the faculty to provide training and ongoing academic development for teaching academics, specifically, to provide advice on curriculum design, including the design of appropriate teaching and learning activities.

Sufficient resources

The discipline-specific adjunct model clearly offers several pedagogical strengths, but designing a content-based course in an unfamiliar discipline is extremely time consuming and resource intensive. In the program described above, the EAP specialists attended all the lectures and subject tutorials, read the core texts and adapted these to design weekly activities for students. For each weekly EAP tutorial, they report having spent between four and six hours on materials development and preparation (which does not include time spent attending lectures, tutorials and meetings). The success of the program relied heavily on adequate resources. Without the resources to support time spent analysing architecture texts, attending lectures and liaising with the discipline academics, it would have been extremely difficult for the language specialists to develop content-based and highly relevant materials and exercises.

While we argue in this book for the benefits of adopting a highly discipline-specific approach to English language development in higher education, we acknowledge that there are limitations to its broader applicability. The language specialists in the case study above used a diagnostic written exercise to select students most in need of further language development. Due to the resource constraints, the program was limited to students assessed as having very poor writing skills, although it is likely that there were many other students in the architecture course who would have benefited from participating in the English language tutorial program. Despite a common belief among language specialists that students would need to continue developing their English language skills throughout their course, this course was only a 12-week semester program.

Summary

If all students with English as an additional language are to be given opportunities and adequate support to develop their English language proficiency during their studies, sufficient funding and resources need to be allocated for the development of integrated, discipline-based English language programs.

The importance of developing English language skills in a disciplinary context has been emphasised by numerous authors (for example, Bruce 2002; Hutchings 2006; Hyland 2000, 2003; Mackiewicz 2004). However, despite a small shift towards discipline-specific programs in English for academic purposes in the past decade, in most Australian higher education institutions the majority of English language support programs, even those that claim to be broadly discipline-based, are extracurricular, that is, peripheral to the core teaching and learning activities taking place in students' courses. In this chapter we have argued for the importance of a discipline-specific approach to English language development that is based on the course content and focused on tasks specific to the discipline in which the students are studying, an approach that acknowledges that language and content are not separate, but rather are closely connected.

If we are to be effective in assisting students with English as an additional language develop the kinds of English language skills necessary for success in higher education courses and beyond, language teaching has to be brought into the mainstream disciplinary curricula. While we are not suggesting widespread implementation of the kind of resource-intensive adjunct program described in this chapter, higher education institutions do need to rethink current practices in English language provision and do more to support the discipline-specific language learning needs of students. Doing this well requires a whole of course approach, in which language development is seen as an ongoing process from entry to exit. To make genuine progress in this area, reforms in curriculum design, and particularly assessment, seem essential. The following chapter examines issues concerning academics' assessment of language and disciplinary learning in higher education.

CHAPTER 5

CURRICULUM DESIGN AND ASSESSMENT OF ENGLISH LANGUAGE PROFICIENCY IN THE DISCIPLINES

The increased diversity of students entering higher education in the past decade has, as explained in the introductory chapter, caused numerous challenges for academic teaching staff and has necessitated a rethinking of curriculum design to support the English language development of students with English as an additional language (Stefani 2004). English language work has to take place within disciplinary teaching and learning as part of the students' core curricula. This necessarily means incorporating English language learning outcomes into the design of curricula and assessment of disciplinary learning. This is a challenging area and one in which the role of academics as disciplinary experts and curriculum designers is crucial.

This chapter discusses the way in which curriculum design can take account of the need to develop English language proficiency. In doing so, it focuses largely on the topic of assessment and the role of academic teaching staff in supporting the development of ELP through their practices. Why the focus on assessment? Because we know from research that assessment plays a crucial role in influencing and driving student learning (Biggs & Tang 2007; Boud 1999; Joughin 2008; Race 2004; Ramsden 2003). This is partly due to the impact of the 'backwash' effect on student learning (Havnes 2004) with suggestions that this has a greater impact on what is learned than do 'formal curricula and teaching methods themselves' (Biggs 1996, p. 5). As Holroyd (2000, p. 43) asserts:

[English Language Standards in Higher Education

> The single most effective way of enhancing learning within higher education is through the improvement of assessment procedures. Assessment is at the core of the academic role of educator.

If assessment is so important in influencing the way students learn, it makes sense that an effective way to encourage EAL students to work on developing their ELP is to clearly communicate its importance through curriculum design and assessment. Language experts agree about the importance of including ELP development in mainstream disciplinary curricula (including assessment). The attitude of those academics who design curricula and teach students is less clear, however. What are academics' views or beliefs about the importance of ELP in the disciplines? Do they assess ELP as part of disciplinary learning? If so, how? Drawing on Baik's study (2010) of academics' beliefs and practices in assessing EAL students' disciplinary learning in higher education, these questions are explored in this chapter. Practical considerations in designing curriculum and assessment that balance the acquisition and development of disciplinary content knowledge with the development of ELP are also discussed.

The literature on assessing ELP in disciplinary learning

There are many ways to assess student performance. The most common approach in many disciplines is to require students to produce written tasks, including essays, reports and extended responses in exams (Dunworth 2008). Writing is viewed by higher education institutions as playing a significant role in the development of understanding and knowledge. It is also seen as an important way for students to demonstrate their academic achievement. Consequently, the ability of students to write has a huge impact on their academic success in many courses. Within this context, and despite plentiful literature on the assessment of ELP in the fields of applied linguistics, language testing and teaching English as a second language (TESOL), little is known about how ELP in the form of writing is assessed by academics.

When we consider the available evidence on the assessment of EAL students' writing by academics, three key approaches are prominent.

The first looks at academics' perceptions of EAL students' writing problems and academic literacy skills (Casanave & Hubbard 1992; Jenkins, Jordan, & Weiland 1993; Johns 1991; Leki 1995; Zhu 2004). The second focuses on the tolerance and reaction of academic teaching staff to errors in writing and their perception of the frequency of particular errors (Janopoulos 1992; Roberts & Cimasko 2008; Santos 1988; Vann, Lorenz, & Meyer 1991). The third looks at the decisions made by academics when they mark EAL writing (Cumming, Kantor, & Powers 2002; Sheehan 2002; Vaughan 1991). The majority of studies focus on the deficiencies or errors in the writing of EAL students. Common descriptors for the writing of EAL students include 'problems' Zhu (2004), 'weaknesses' and even 'academic illiteracy' (John 1991), with particular references to restricted disciplinary vocabulary and inability to provide relevant examples (John 1991). The literature highlights different beliefs about the relationship and interplay between language (grammar, mechanics, vocabulary and syntax) and content (idea development, organisation, support, logic, relevance and quantity) (Sakyi 2000; Weigle 2002; Weigle et al. 2003).

What is less clear is the role that discipline plays in the attitudes of academics towards EAL writing (Roberts & Cimasko 2008; Santos 1988; Vann et al. 1984). This is a crucial piece of information. Without gathering insights about the way in which academics in different disciplinary areas view the written work of EAL students it is not possible to determine priorities in the teaching and learning of academic writing in those disciplines. It is easy to imagine that disciplinary differences exist, and that academics' beliefs will have an impact on their practice (Pajares 1992). Concrete evidence is needed to go beyond simplistic assumptions, however. In this chapter, data collected from a study with academics at a leading Australian higher education institution are used to indicate variations between the attitudes of staff in different disciplines (Baik 2010).

Disciplinary differences in assessing English language proficiency

Research was conducted with academic teaching staff at an Australian higher education institution (Baik 2010). The institution had a large and diverse student population of more than 42 000, at least one-third of whom would be considered EAL students. Academic staff from seven disciplines were surveyed: economics and commerce, law, engineering, architecture, arts/humanities, health sciences and science. Participants varied in age, years of teaching experience and academic seniority, reflecting the diversity commonly found among academic teaching staff in higher education institutions around the world.

Participants were asked to report on the importance of particular features of academic writing and how ELP factored in their assessment of disciplinary learning. Table 5.1 provides a summary of responses for teaching staff in three disciplines and highlights the variations between them. It is clear that for the majority of academics (95.3 per cent) in the study, the ability to write well was considered to be very important. Although close to all the respondents were in agreement that content-related and discourse-level features such as structuring ideas and critical

Table 5.1: Features of writing academics consider very important

Feature of writing	Commerce (n=24) % within discipline	Law (n=21) % within discipline	Engineering (n=19) % within discipline
Structure of ideas	95.8	95.2	89.5
Logical connections between ideas	87.5	95.2	84.2
Critical thinking/analysis	75.0	95.2	94.7
Use of sources	41.7	76.2	41.7
Paragraph organisation	54.2	57.1	42.1
Evidence of wide reading/research	29.2	61.9	36.8
Disciplinary writing style	41.7	66.7	15.8
Appropriate vocabulary	33.3	61.9	10.5
Correct spelling	37.5	42.9	26.3
Correct grammar and sentences	29.2	57.1	10.5
Correct punctuation	29.2	38.1	10.5
Ability to express ideas in original language	25.0	33.3	21.1

thinking are important, there was less agreement about word- and sentence-level features and disciplinary style. For example, 61.9 per cent of respondents from the discipline of law considered 'appropriate vocabulary' to be very important in the assessment of learning in contrast to 33.3 per cent from commerce and just 10.5 per cent from engineering. There were also disciplinary differences in the weight academics placed on writing skills, a finding which is consistent with a number of studies in the USA (for example, Cumming, Kantor, & Power 2002; Janopoulos 1992; Vann et al. 1984) that show that academics' disciplinary background has a greater impact on assessment practices than other characteristics.

Interviews with participants highlighted the value placed by academic staff on discourse-level characteristics. Rather than focusing on word- or sentence-level characteristics, 'clarity of written expression' is viewed as of crucial importance. What is less clear is how different individuals interpret this term. Quotes from two academics provide some insight into the divergence of opinions. An academic from the discipline of commerce states:

> Their ability to communicate their research is essential. Grammar and vocabulary [are] part of this ability and, therefore, [they] should be assessed.

This indicates an interpretation of 'clarity of written expression' which takes account of grammar and vocabulary. In contrast, an academic from law suggests that precision in the choice of words is of greatest importance:

> Clear expression, precision in word choice from a wide vocabulary; I will expect them to have a broad vocabulary that they're drawing from and to show me that they understand distinction and discrimination.

These findings support our argument for integrating English language development within disciplinary learning. There is evidence, however, that this is not done in any systematic fashion across the different disciplines. This means that universities may not have a systematic approach to ensuring the English language standards of their graduates.

The role of academic teaching staff

If academics from different disciplines view ELP differently, how do they see their roles in supporting EAL students to develop English language writing skills? What approaches (if any) do they use in supporting students to develop academic writing skills? If the English skills of an enrolling EAL student are merely a starting point, who has the responsibility for ensuring that each student continues to develop their English language skills for success in their studies and beyond? There are indications that even when academic teaching staff view EAL students' English language skills as vital to performance in a discipline, they are constrained in tackling any problems they detect. As one academic states:

> I believe that communication skills are important for undergraduates ... but our large classes do not permit us the time to comment on their grammar and vocabulary. As a result, a significant proportion of students graduate with deplorable language.

As the quote indicates, a lack of time to address the English language needs of EAL students, and a perception that it is not their responsibility, are commonly reported by academic teaching staff, who mainly focus on their role as disciplinary specialists. Nevertheless, many staff members do adopt a number of strategies to support their EAL students, particularly in improving their writing skills. A typology of academics' responses to EAL writing is presented in Table 5.2. The approach taken reflects their espoused theories about their role as teachers. Those who see their role as assisting students to develop their English language and writing skills tend to provide high levels of intervention, such as providing detailed feedback on drafts of written work or correcting most or all linguistic errors. In contrast, those academic teaching staff who believe that it is not their role as discipline experts to assist students – either because they believe they lack the expertise to 'teach writing' or because they believe it is the students' responsibility to develop their language skills (or that they should already have these skills) – tend to provide 'indirect' forms of support such as advising students to 'seek help with their language'.

Interestingly, Baik (2010) found little association between discipline and the level of intervention provided. She did, however,

Curriculum design and assessment

Table 5.2: Typology of academic practices in responding to students' writing

Practices	Examples	
Giving overall general feedback on student work.	Giving general feedback pointing out that students need to work on their language and/or writing skills.	**Minimal intervention (indirect support)**
Advising students to seek help with writing and/or language development.	Giving feedback to advise students to seek help from the language and academic support units. Suggesting that students seek proofreading assistance from native-speaking peers for future assessment tasks.	
Organising a workshop on writing for students.	Arranging a workshop with a language specialist to review aspects of academic writing for the next assignment.	
Making some corrections and pointing out specific problems or areas that need improvement.	Correcting some of the errors (usually on the first few pages only), and then commenting on areas that need improvement. Making a list of types of errors or problems with writing and language use and asking students to resubmit corrected assignment.	
Correcting most or all errors as feedback and suggesting alternative expression.	Making corrections to most or all linguistic errors throughout the student's text and highlighting awkward phrases and/or sentences and suggesting alternative expressions.	
Reading drafts of work and providing detailed feedback.	Providing extensive writing and/or language support though careful proofreading and editing of several drafts of work before submission of final assignment.	
Providing intensive individual support to students in all stages of the writing process.	Providing individual consultations with students to assist them at various stages of assignment writing, from reading and formulating ideas to structuring information, to proofreading and editing. Examples of this only occurred in relatively small classes with fewer than 30 students.	**High intervention (direct support)**

85

find a correlation with the number of years of experience, with more experienced teaching staff providing higher levels of intervention. It would appear that experienced teaching staff view assessments as both summative and formative, both certifying student achievement and as a vehicle for providing formative feedback.

Attitudes towards their responsibilities in supporting English language improvements among EAL students inevitably influence the attitudes of academics to assessment, and in particular, the allocation of marks for written expression. Approximately one-third of the respondents in Baik's study reported explicitly assessing written expression by allocating a small proportion (between 5 and 10 per cent) of marks to written expression (for example, spelling, punctuation, syntax).

Explanations given for explicitly awarding marks for written expression include the impact of language use on the quality of the written task and the ability of academics to understand and assess the piece of work. An academic in the discipline of law commented:

> Standards of expression are listed in the marking criteria because they affect comprehensibility of the information and argument presented by the student.

Similarly an academic in engineering explained that he tried to separate our language usage (5 per cent) from content for marking purposes, stating:

> If there are excessive errors or grammar is so bad that the arguments presented are not communicated at all, then the 5 per cent is lost.

References were also made to the expectations of a particular profession. An architecture academic commented that 'the aim is to produce articulate future professionals'. An academic from the discipline of engineering noted:

> A small number of marks are normally given for presentation and clarity, including grammar, spelling, and concise expression, reflecting the quality of writing expected in professional engineering practice.

Assessing language and content

The finding that many academics report trying to ignore language factors when assessing student work raises an important question regarding whether it is possible to assess the quality of ideas without assessing how language is used to communicate those ideas. In other words, is it possible to truly separate language from content for assessment?

For the most part, academics report seeing writing and language as separate from disciplinary content knowledge, thus English language proficiency occupies a subordinate role to content in the assessment practices of most academics in this study. These academics perhaps do not see writing and the role of language as complex or multidimensional, but rather as discrete components. There are noticeable disciplinary differences, with most academics from the science-based disciplines reporting that they either ignore the quality of written expression in their assessment of student work, or that they allocate a small proportion of marks for language usage. For these academics, the focus is squarely on demonstration of (technical) content knowledge. Sometimes this means adding the number of points made by the student or identifying whether the expected content is there.

The academics from the humanities believe that language performs a vital role in constructing content and in demonstrating understanding of content knowledge. As one humanities academic notes: 'Written expression is a highly significant qualitative consideration in assessment.' As do these academics, we argue that language and content are deeply connected and cannot be separated when assessing complex written work. Reed et al. (2003, p. 22), for example, emphasise the difficulties of assessing language separately from the other assessment criteria. They write that

> Language and cognition are intimately bound up and poor use of language affects students' overall performance ... it is not possible to formulate an argument or to provide a nuanced interpretation of the data without control of the language.

Turner (2004, p. 104) also argues that students can only show their understanding of the content by being able to manipulate language. In other words, 'language proficiency is as important as content knowledge'. She adds that the 'language–content dichotomy', which is hierarchical, falsely deems content to be more important than language. She adds:

> This subordinate positioning [of language] is bolstered by the assumption ... that language proficiency is only a pre-requisite and not an ongoing process of development linked to what is being studied.

While the nature of higher education assessment tasks and related marking criteria appear to focus primarily on content knowledge (Leki 2007), we know that in terms of written assessment, language usage and written expression affect the clarity of the message conveyed and thus academics' reading and assessment of the work (Vann, Meyer, & Lorenz 1984; Zhu 2004). The accurate use of language is fundamental to the adequate demonstration and expression of content knowledge, from the way ideas are logically organised and connected to present an argument, to the choice and use of appropriate words, to the way meaning is built within and between sentences. As Hyland (2007) notes, learning to write involves learning to use language. Students would benefit by learning how to use language to perform a variety of discipline-specific writing functions. By incorporating English language development in disciplinary teaching and learning, students would develop the knowledge and skills to use language effectively in demonstrating their understanding of the disciplinary content and to convey meaning clearly.

If we are to make real progress in developing students' English language proficiency, we need to adopt a whole of course approach in which English language work is embedded in disciplinary learning. The role of the academic as curriculum developer, teacher and assessor seems crucial in this approach. We are not suggesting that the best approach is one of high intervention, especially given the increasing pressures on academics' workload. Rather, we argue that English language proficiency should be included – according to academics' particular departmental or disciplinary context – as an important component of curriculum design, particularly in assessment practice.

Curriculum design and assessment

Designing curriculum for English language proficiency development

A well-designed curriculum that places importance on ELP development would include reference to ELP in the explicit learning objectives (in addition to the objectives related to disciplinary content and skills), have teaching and learning activities that encourage the development of ELP and assessment tasks that evaluate the extent to which students have met the intended learning outcomes. For most subjects or courses, objectives related to ELP will only account for one or two of the explicit learning objectives.

According to leading higher education scholar John Biggs, a well-designed curriculum is one that is constructively aligned (Biggs 1996; Biggs & Tang 2007). This means one in which learning objectives or intended learning outcomes, teaching and learning approaches and assessment are aligned. Constructive alignment is based on two fundamental principles:

1. that learners use their own activity to construct knowledge (based on constructivist learning theory
2. that intended learning outcomes should be 'activated in the teaching' through the teaching and learning activities and assessment (Biggs & Tang 2007, p. 52).

Developing students' ELP in a constructively aligned curriculum (Biggs 2003) means:
- having specific English language skills as explicit learning objectives (intended learning outcomes)
- designing (perhaps in collaboration with a language specialist) teaching and learning activities that help students develop these English language skills
- explicitly assessing how well students have achieved the intended learning outcomes.

An example of learning objectives that are aligned with teaching and learning activities and assessment is presented in Figure 5.1.

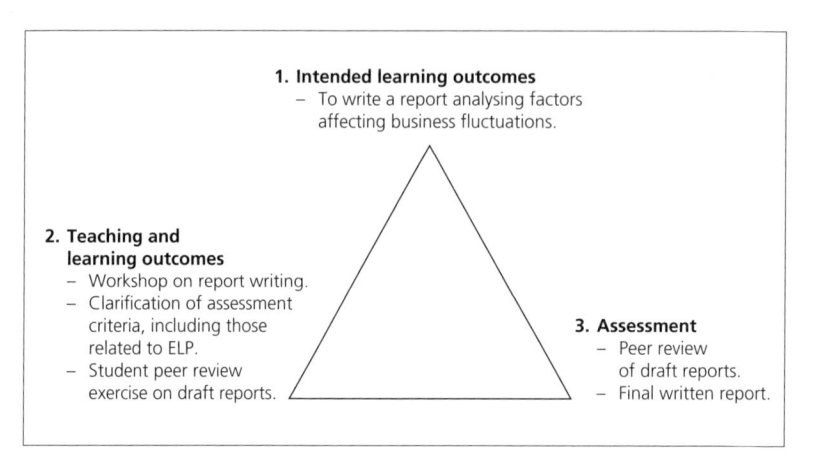

```
                    1. Intended learning outcomes
                       – To write a report analysing factors
                         affecting business fluctuations.

2. Teaching and
   learning outcomes
   – Workshop on report writing.
   – Clarification of assessment
     criteria, including those            3. Assessment
     related to ELP.                      – Peer review
   – Student peer review                    of draft reports.
     exercise on draft reports.           – Final written report.
```

Figure 5.1: Curriculum designed to develop written English language proficiency in an Economics course

Using assessment to encourage ELP development

> The students are motivated by the assessment. I don't want to generalise but if it's included, often they come in to see me and if they bring in a marking criteria sheet, which includes 'creative expression, fluency', those types of things as criteria, then they do take it very seriously. They will say to me, 'Is my English okay? What can I do?' If it's not there, you can't blame them.
>
> Academic, Commerce

This quote captures what we know from the literature about the role of assessment in sending the right messages to students about the importance of developing ELP as part of their higher education. As the findings of Baik's study (2010) show, ELP is often implicitly assessed or ignored by academics when evaluating student work, yet we know that the majority of academics believe ELP to be very important in their disciplines and in the professions. The study conducted by O'Loughlin and Arkoudis (2009) in an Australian university showed that some students complete a professional

Curriculum design and assessment

course having had few opportunities (or requirements) to develop their writing skills. In other words, the assessment tasks students completed during their course did not require the development or demonstration of written English language skills. This led to a decline in written language proficiency as assessed by the IELTS test (compared with entry test scores) for some students, and no improvement in writing skills for others.

So what can be done to use assessment as a vehicle to promote ELP development? Table 5.4 lists nine suggestions for enhancing assessment practice to support ELP development.

Table 5.3: Assessment practices to support the development of English language proficiency

For academic teaching staff	
1	Emphasise the importance of ELP through explicit and published assessment criteria that align with the learning objectives of subjects and the course overall.
2	Clarify expectations in relation to ELP and the standards required to complete the assessment task.
3	Work with language specialists to develop teaching and learning activities that feed into the assessment task and help students develop their ELP.
4	Use formative assessment tasks that focus on ELP development where students have opportunities to learn from feedback from peers (and teacher).
5	Explore possibilities for using peer and self-assessment to encourage self-regulated language learning.

For department leaders	
6	Include explicit reference to ELP in published course graduate attributes; encourage and support collaboration between content experts and language specialists to explore practical ways of assessing ELP as part of disciplinary learning.
7	Engage in whole of course curriculum mapping and review to ensure that ELP is developed and assessed throughout the course.
8	Facilitate discussion among teaching staff to share ideas for assessment design, examine issues related to the assessment of EAL student work and develop a shared understanding of minimum standards of ELP attainment for the degree.
9	Provide opportunities and incentives for staff to engage in professional development activities on curriculum design and assessment for developing students' ELP.

Clearly, there is not a one size fits all approach to facilitating the ongoing English language development of students with English as an additional language; however, including ELP in curriculum design and assessment seems a logical starting point and one in which academics' disciplinary and departmental contexts can be considered.

Summary

Academics are fairly united in their view that ELP is important, although in terms of writing, there are clear discipline-based differences in their beliefs about what constitutes good writing. While academics espouse that written language skills are crucial in the discipline and professions, this belief is not necessarily borne out in their curriculum or assessment practices, which raises concerns about what kinds of messages (about the importance of English language) students are receiving from academics' assessment practice. As Biggs and Tang (2007, p. 16) assert, 'Assessment practices must send the right signals to students about what they should be learning and how they should be learning it'.

Assessment practices must encourage the development of important English language skills required not only for success in academic pursuits, but also for successfully communicating beyond the higher education institution, particularly in the workplace. While it seems clear that adequate English language proficiency is essential for the professional workplace, it is less clear whose role it is to ensure that students graduate with the necessary proficiency. What is the role of institutions in ensuring that students have acquired the level of ELP necessary to function successfully in the workplace? What can students, the community and employers expect from graduates in terms of their ELP? These questions are explored in later chapters.

CHAPTER 6

DESIGNING CURRICULA TO ENHANCE INTERACTION

Assessment of learning in higher education contexts is mainly concerned with written work. As a result, most of the discussion about English standards in higher education has concentrated on developing students' written English language ability. Far less attention has been given to the development of students' spoken English language. Part of the reason for this is that it is often assumed that students will demonstrate similar levels of ELP in both written and spoken language ability. This is not necessarily the case. Research has found that English language development is neither linear nor predictable (O'Loughlin & Arkoudis 2009), with graduating students attaining different levels of ELP in spoken and written ability.

Enhancing opportunities for students to improve their speaking ability is important, because it enables EAL students to engage more fully with their classroom activities and contribute effectively to group discussions. More importantly, it allows students to express their disciplinary understanding in English and engage in their learning environment. There are benefits for domestic students as well. It offers opportunities for them to develop their intercultural communication skills, which are important because employers seek graduates who can communicate effectively in the workplace. The challenges for higher education institutions are to increase opportunities for diverse student groups to interact and develop their social English language skills. This chapter discusses approaches to enhancing interaction between diverse student groups within teaching and learning contexts. This links to the discussion in Chapter 8 concerning graduates' exit to employment.

Fostering interactions between international and domestic students

Increasingly, higher education institutions are required to ensure that their graduates have the necessary knowledge and skills to work in their chosen professions. Interpersonal communication skills are considered important attributes for graduates to have, especially as many will work with people from diverse cultural and linguistic backgrounds. This is true for all graduates, not only for EAL students.

Research by O'Loughlin and Arkoudis (2009) investigated factors that influence international EAL students' ELP improvement in higher education. Their study involved 63 students who were studying business and economics courses in one Australian university. Using pre- and post-course IELTS results, one of the main findings of the study was that while most of the students improved in one or more of their English skills (that is, listening, speaking, reading and writing) very few students showed improvement in all skill areas. Interestingly, their research also found that results in listening, reading and writing tended to cluster together, but were not strongly correlated with speaking results. In other words, 'students tended to improve more or less in speaking than they did in listening, reading and writing' (p. 131). Not surprisingly, one of the main factors influencing speaking ability was the extent to which the students had opportunities to interact with English speakers.

Yet opportunities for international EAL students and domestic students to interact outside of classes are limited. Many domestic students have part-time employment and other commitments that keep them away from campus. It seems that if there is to be more interaction between domestic and international students, most of it will have to take place within the formal curriculum in the classroom. Findings from Arkoudis et al.'s (2010) study, which involved interviews with academic staff and students from a variety of disciplines at three Australian universities, suggest that there are a number of obstacles to student interaction for the academics interviewed. These include lack of time to foster interaction because of large class sizes, the large volume of content to be covered and lack of planning in the curriculum. These obstacles inhibit academics' ability to ensure that there is adequate time for peer interaction in their teaching. In relation to student

Designing curricula to enhance interaction

learning, staff and students identified a number of challenges for interaction, including some students' English language skills, work commitments, limited time spent on campus and lack of common ground between domestic and international students who differ in their linguistic and cultural backgrounds as well as in their previous learning experiences.

Paradoxically, one of the biggest obstacles for enhancing interaction between international and domestic students is international students' weak social communicative language ability. A number of the academics interviewed for the Arkoudis et al. study observed that many international students were generally shy about speaking to domestic students because of their perceived weaker English language skills. A few academics believed that international students' 'shyness' was due to their different educational and cultural experiences.

Many international and local students indicated that even when there were opportunities for them to interact, it was often very difficult. One student referred to this as the lack of 'common ground'. When asked about what made the interaction difficult and whether there were opportunities to interact, the majority of both international and domestic students interviewed admitted that everybody remained with their own group and did not want to cross their cultural comfort zones. Many of the domestic students commented on the difficulties from their perspective:

> [We] stick with friends from high schools because you can relate to each other, such as talking about sport. International students don't follow Australian sport, so there is no common ground to talk about things.

Another domestic student made a similar observation:

> My friends and I talk about a TV show and that excludes international students ... also popular culture and movies. I just don't interact with them enough because we have no stories we can share.

A third domestic student reported a different experience. He found that it was easier for him to interact with some international students because he could speak their language. The language offered the common ground for their interaction:

> I seek out international students who speak Mandarin. It helps to improve my skills in the language and I explain things to them in English. It's good for me and for them.

It was apparent from the domestic student interviews that a lack of common ground and a lack of social communicative language ability were the main obstacles to interaction. Many of the international students voiced similar concerns regarding a lack of common ground. Typical comments were:

> No common topics with local students, they talk about TV shows and celebrities. We don't know much about it.

A few students indicated that perhaps subject learning could bridge the interaction gap between local and international students:

> ... sometimes you don't know what to say, after you talk about the weather, there is no common topic. The tutorials and classes are very important to create this conversation starter.

Most of the student comments involved outside classroom activities, although it appeared that there is potential for fostering 'common ground' through interaction within teaching and learning. Both domestic and international EAL students lacked the necessary communicative ability to negotiate intercultural difference that could lead to finding common areas of interest.

The following section presents a framework and examples for enhancing interaction among diverse students in higher education. The work was developed for a project that explored the benefits of, and obstacles to, interaction among students from diverse cultural and linguistic backgrounds, and identified examples of practice that could enhance that interaction within the teaching and learning environment. Support for the project on which the material in this chapter is based was provided by the Australian Learning and Teaching Council (now the Office for Learning and Teaching), an initiative of the Department of Education, Employment and Workplace Relations.

The interaction for learning framework

The interaction for learning framework is a conceptual framework underpinned by five core principles. It:
- engages students from diverse cultural and linguistic backgrounds in the learning context in a variety of ways
- embeds interaction in curriculum planning and links to teaching, learning and assessment
- acknowledges and capitalises on student diversity as a resource for learning and teaching
- promotes peer engagement through curriculum-based activities
- recognises the variety of ways that interaction can be used across different learning contexts.

The interaction for learning framework presented in Figure 7.1 consists of six dimensions that interact with each other. The dimension planning interaction, in the centre, connects the other five dimensions: creating environments for interaction, supporting

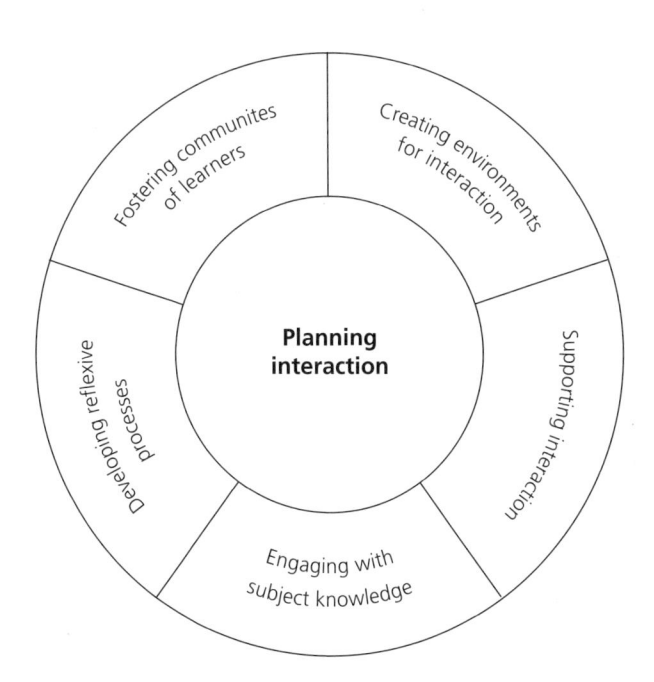

Figure 6.1: The interaction for learning framework

interaction, engaging with subject knowledge, developing reflexive processes and fostering communities of learners.

Planning interaction

Planning for interaction is the first important stage in fostering peer engagement among students from diverse backgrounds. Planning interaction involves incorporating it as part of the course or subject design as well as linking the objectives of intercultural interaction with the course or subject learning outcomes and the assessment process (De Vita 2002; Leask 2009). This means developing relevant learning tasks that require interaction and giving students clear guidelines about the objectives of peer learning, assessment processes and expected learning outcomes.

Planning for interaction means creating the need for peer interaction in formal learning through course design. To do this requires academics to design peer interaction activities that align with assessment tasks and student learning outcomes. Formalising peer interaction within academic courses can be achieved in a number of ways. These include:

- incorporating interaction among students from diverse backgrounds as a course objective and making this explicit in published course outlines
- designing and structuring teaching and learning activities that require students to communicate and engage with peers from diverse backgrounds
- designing assessment tasks that align with the objective of student interaction and peer engagement. These tasks may, for instance, require students to work with peers from different backgrounds to consider or compare different perspectives on an issue or topic, and then critically reflect on the group process.

Examples from practice

Below are several examples that illustrate how academics from various disciplines have planned and incorporated interaction in their course design. The strategies adopted will depend largely on the specific institutional and disciplinary teaching and learning context in which academics work. Each one demonstrates the

Designing curricula to enhance interaction

way in which setting up situations where students from different backgrounds need to interact with each other can lead to a number of positive outcomes.

EXAMPLE: PROBLEM SOLVING IN ENGINEERING

An engineering lecturer structures his course in such a way that requires problem solving in small groups from the start of the course. Some of the group activities are assessed tasks. The aim of such joint tasks is to foster peer interaction and capitalise on a range of abilities and diverse experiences students bring to the class. Because students are told to form groups based on a diverse set of skills and experiences, the interaction and mix of students happens quickly, from the first class.

EXAMPLE: TEAM-BASED LEARNING IN LAW

A lecturer in law structures the learning activities in her course so that students work in syndicates or teams for the whole semester. Rather than allowing students to form their own teams, she allocates them to syndicates to ensure that there is a mix of international and domestic students in each team. All class discussions are based on the syndicate groups so students soon become used to working together with their team members. One of the assessment tasks requires the teams to conduct research for a group presentation and to write a report. After a few weeks of working in the same teams, students build good working relationships with their peers and some form study groups for exam preparation.

EXAMPLE: PROJECT-BASED LEARNING IN MARKETING

A marketing lecturer structures the first half of her subject around a large project that involves students conducting research and coming up with a marketing strategy. Students work in pairs to interview (in depth) two students from different cultural backgrounds as research for designing an advertising campaign targeting young people in those students' countries. An Australian-born student could, for example, pair with a Korean international student and decide to design an advertising campaign for young people in Hong Kong and Singapore. The project requires integration of course materials or content and data collected from interviews. The assessment is based on students' presentation of their campaign and a written report.

Creating environments for interaction

Students feel more comfortable forming friendship groups and interacting with others from similar backgrounds (Dunne 2009). This is true for international students as well as for domestic students. As we have discussed already, however, it is essential for students to interact with those from different backgrounds if they are to develop intercultural awareness. At the same time, EAL students will struggle to improve their spoken English if they only interact with other EAL students. It is therefore very important to find ways to bring students from different backgrounds together. While it may appear that students are reluctant to move outside their familiar social groupings in classrooms, feedback from students suggests that they expect and value opportunities to have meaningful, structured learning and social interactions with peers from different backgrounds. The main aims of creating environments for interaction are to:

- set up teaching and learning conditions for effective interaction from the start of the subject
- create opportunities within learning and teaching activities for interaction
- encourage students to move out of their regular social groups
- develop students' confidence in interacting with students from diverse cultural and linguistic backgrounds
- provide EAL students with opportunities to improve their spoken English.

Designing teaching and learning activities at the early stage of a subject can create a learning environment in which peer interaction is considered important to developing understandings about the subject material and in achieving desired learning outcomes. This establishes a context in which EAL students have ample opportunities to practice and improve their spoken English. Activities in this dimension begin to lay the groundwork for future interaction, and imply that these need to be planned throughout the duration of the subject. A number of strategies can be used to create a positive environment for interaction. Some of these are outlined below.

Facilitating interactive activities from the first session

The first session is crucial to how the tone is set for the rest of the semester. It is important for academics to create a warm, supportive atmosphere in which interaction among students is encouraged and expected. To achieve this, it is important to devote time in the first class to introductions. This may involve asking students to introduce themselves and telling their peers about their background, interests or pastimes. It could also involve facilitating several icebreaker activities as start-ups, in which students talk to each other or work together to complete a task or solve a small problem. Establishing an expectation that students will interact with each other from the first class sets up the right conditions for ongoing communication, optimising opportunities for EAL students to speak in English during class.

Icebreakers can be a useful way of creating a warm, informal atmosphere for interaction. They can help students feel comfortable with each other and create openness and trust. Academics can ask students to talk to another student for five minutes, learn three interesting facts about the person and report back to the whole class, a simple activity that can be useful in helping students become acquainted with others in their class and thereby weaken barriers to interaction. This, in turn, will assist to create a learning environment that welcomes multiple perspectives and stimulates interaction.

Beginning each class with a short peer-learning activity

This is perhaps easier in a small group teaching environment, such as a tutorial or practical class, but it can also be done in large lectures. A very useful starting activity is to ask students, in pairs or small groups, to spend three to five minutes reviewing the main points from the previous lecture or tutorial. Alternatively, academics may like to provide one or two review questions or problems for students to discuss or solve. These kinds of activities have several benefits for academics as well as students: they take take only a few minutes to do and, from the start of the lesson, require students to interact to perform a relevant and useful task. It also enables academics to evaluate students' understanding of important material covered in the previous session. Discussions based on the topic of classes also ensure that EAL students have the opportunity to make use of disciplinary concepts and terminology in conversation with others, helping them gain confidence to use terms which may be unfamiliar.

Encouraging students to move out of their regular social groups

Allocating seating or asking students to work in a group with different students can be effective strategies for facilitating interaction among students from diverse backgrounds, although is easier to achieve in small class environments than in large lecture theatres. Academics can prompt interactions between students from different cultural backgrounds by giving them a targeted task which requires them to consider different approaches to a problem or situation. An alternative is to challenge students to explain to others what benefits they would bring to a group. If EAL students are not confident in spoken English, creating situations in which they are obliged to speak to their peers can help them to overcome some of their anxiety. And with repeated practice, confidence is likely to increase.

Supporting interaction

The primary aim of supporting interaction is to assist students to understand the purpose and value of interaction and help them develop the skills they need for it. Many students, regardless of their background, do not recognise the benefits to their learning of interacting with peers from diverse cultural and linguistic backgrounds. Academic staff may need to clearly articulate the benefits of peer learning, support effective student interaction by setting expectations and rules for respectful interaction and help students to develop the skills necessary for effective interaction and collaborative learning (Boud 2001).

To benefit from peer learning, students need to develop the communication and interpersonal skills necessary for effective peer interaction. There are numerous ways academics can help prepare students for effective interaction and learning across diverse cultural groups. A number of suggestions are presented below.

Designing curricula to enhance interaction

Setting clear expectations

Being clear about the expectations for peer interaction and group work is an important part of supporting peer learning. Students benefit from learning about the purpose of peer interaction and the potential benefits of engaging with peers from diverse backgrounds. What kinds of group activities will students be expected to participate in? How will these enhance their learning? In other words, why should students actively participate in these activities? How can students interact effectively? What are the expectations or rules for interaction? Remind students about respectful ways of communicating, including taking turns and acknowledging diverse perspectives. It may be necessary to provide students with particular insights into the challenges involved in engaging in academic discussions in a language other than their mother tongue.

Facilitating a peer-learning workshop

Facilitating a short workshop on peer learning can be an effective way to help students become familiar with the types of peer activities and group processes they will be engaged in during the semester and over the year. Class time devoted to peer interaction or group work gives students the opportunity to:

- hear about the idea of peer interaction for learning across diverse cultural and linguistic groups
- learn how peer learning processes are consistent with the outcomes of the course
- discuss the expectations and their role in peer learning activities
- set, as a group, the guidelines or rules for peer interaction and group work
- form groups for team projects and start to build rapport with team members
- practise essential communication skills for interaction, including active listening, turn-taking, questioning, negotiating, and giving and receiving feedback
- start to learn how to build upon peers' knowledge and experiences to extend views and co-construct knowledge
- raise questions about group work.

Negotiating the parameters around interaction with each other can be especially useful for EAL students who may be unfamiliar with the unspoken rules and customs around conversation which are embedded in a particular language and cultural context. A lack of familiarity can undermine confidence and impede communication. Peer learning workshops also offer a good opportunity to get students to consider the cultural variations around interaction which are found in different countries and contexts. This can assist those students with the least international exposure to understand why some of their peers may at first seem shy or reluctant to interact.

Providing group work resources for students

In addition to time spent in class setting up and supporting peer interaction, a useful way of supporting group work is to provide a handout or print resources for students. Although the specific strategies and suggestions will vary according to particular course or subjects, the resources could include information and advice that address the following broad questions:

- Why should students interact with their classmates from diverse cultural and linguistic backgrounds? What are the benefits to their learning in doing so?
- How does peer interaction fit with academic expectations and future workplace needs?
- How does peer interaction relate to the course objectives and assessment criteria?
- What are the different forms of peer interaction for learning?
- What are some strategies for working effectively in multicultural groups?
- How can students monitor and evaluate their own progress in developing teamwork skills for working across diverse cultures?

Engaging with subject knowledge

The first three dimensions of the interaction framework (see Figure 6.1) – planning interaction, creating environments for interaction and supporting interaction – are important in preparing students to engage actively in collaborative learning activities. The main purpose of the fourth dimension – engaging with subject knowledge – is to encourage students' engagement with the subject content through peer learning activities and to create a mutually respectful atmosphere and a sense of shared purpose and collaboration. Various structured collaborative activities can be used to promote peer engagement and enable students to learn from each other's knowledge, experiences, cultural norms and values. Students benefit when they are encouraged to explore similar and different perspectives on issues and problems, and to share their diverse experiences. EAL students can gain the fluency they need for employment in their chosen professional field if they practise using the specific language of their discipline. Collaborative activities around subject content are an ideal way to encourage development in spoken disciplinary English. Activities designed to provide these kinds of collaborative learning opportunities include (but are not limited to):

- discussion-based activities that require students to discuss an issue, analyse a case study, present an argument and/or provide examples from their experience
- problem solving activities that require students to pool their knowledge and work together through a problem or set of questions
- group projects that require diverse perspectives and a range of skills
- practical activities that require students to apply technical or practical skills (for example, conducting a chemistry experiment, constructing a model, giving a presentation, preparing an artistic performance, etc.).

The types of peer interaction activities used will depend largely on the learning objectives of the particular topic or session, as well as teaching and learning contexts (including class size and time constraints). Below are four examples to illustrate how academics from different disciplines use various activities to foster peer learning and enhance engagement with subject knowledge.

Academics from a range of disciplines often use small-group discussion activities as a way of facilitating peer interaction in class. To encourage peer learning among students from diverse cultural backgrounds, discussion questions may ask for different perspectives or approaches to examining the issue or problem, or they may require students to present evidence from various perspectives. Some academics regularly ask students to work in pairs to discuss the question before asking them to join another pair of students to consider and compare multiple perspectives. Another strategy used by some academics is to ask students to work with different students each week.

EXAMPLE: DISCUSSION-BASED ACTIVITIES IN SCIENCE

A science academic who teaches first-year students begins each session with a question that students discuss in pairs or groups of three. Throughout the session these students work with their partners (sometimes joining another pair of students) to work through questions. Students are told to work with someone different each week. The academic explains that

> Students can learn so much from each other. When they have to explain something to their partner, you know they understand it, and you can see some people go 'Oh, now I get it' or 'I hadn't thought of that' when they discuss questions with their partner ... And most students really like working with another student that they might not have known previously.

EXAMPLE: GROUP PROJECTS IN MANAGEMENT

In the postgraduate subject Consultancy Workshop, students undertake research projects in teams. This involves students from different cultural backgrounds going together to meet their clients outside the institution and identify their research problems. Each student has a specific major role in the project, but the project requires collaboration in the whole process, from data collection to analysis and reporting. International students are also encouraged to use data or research problems from their own country, so all students have opportunities to be exposed to a situation in different cultures. The lecturer notes that

> Students are very pleased with the experience as they interact with peers and clients from diverse backgrounds and learn about different cultural perspectives.

EXAMPLE: STUDENT PEER REVIEW IN CREATIVE WRITING

In a creative writing class, students are asked to analyse, review and comment on each other's work. The aim is to help to clarify and reinforce students' (reviewers and reviewed) knowledge and understanding of the subject and promote the development of critical thinking and higher order cognitive skills (Pearce, Mulder, & Baik 2009). Through engaging in peer review with a number of students, learners have the opportunity to be exposed to a diversity of perspectives and approaches. As well, students practise

Designing curricula to enhance interaction

and further develop a range of important social and communication skills, including verbal and written communication, negotiation skills and diplomacy (in giving and accepting criticism) (Topping 1998). Because peer reviewing is a complex skill and students need to be guided through the process, the academic conducts a peer review workshop on giving feedback.

Engaging in peer review can enhance group relationships through increased interactivity, self-confidence and empathy for others. The process can also influence students' attitudes about peer learning as they start to see their peers as 'legitimate sources of knowledge' (Gehringer et al. 2005, p. 321) There are a number of resources (see Pearce, Mulder, & Baik 2009) that offer useful suggestions on implementing student peer review.

EXAMPLE: TEAM-BASED LEARNING IN INTERNATIONAL COMMUNICATION

There are numerous variations of team-based learning, but one example of a particular type, developed by Larry Michaelsen, involves the use of a Readiness Assurance Test at the beginning of each session. One academic in an international communication class uses this strategy in his teaching. Based on the week's readings, students are required to individually complete the Readiness Assurance Test at the beginning of each class, then, in intercultural teams that complete the quiz again, discuss and debate the questions to arrive at team answers to the questions. Usually, students will find that their team arrives at more correct answers than any individual did when they did the quiz alone. The lecturer explains:

> Peer teaching is naturalised, it becomes part and parcel. All students are required to contribute and they interact effectively immediately because they are compelled to do so.

Developing reflexive processes

The fifth dimension of the interaction framework (see Figure 7.1) – developing reflexive processes – aims to promote higher levels of interaction and cognitive engagement, and enhance students' critical thinking and reflection on their learning. Peer interaction for learning requires students to confront any differences in each other's current understanding of a topic as well as their differing attitudes or perspectives. When students are exposed to alternative perceptions and conflicting views they are motivated to continue the discussion in order to resolve the cognitive conflict. Through explaining and defending their views to their group, those conflicts can be reconciled, which enables students to arrive at negotiated meanings (King 2002, p. 37). The reflective process during peer learning thus encourages students to become more open to critical thinking.

In addition, peer learning is enriched when learners take a step back and reflect on the learning process. Reflecting on their own role and contribution to a group project, for example, encourages students to develop self-assessment skills important for lifelong learning. Students can also be encouraged to reflect on the overall group process and to evaluate the strengths and weaknesses (or areas in need of improvement) of their group's approach. When learners share their reflections and exchange ideas about their learning, their sense of empathy and encouragement grows, as does their understanding of each other (Welikala & Watkins 2008, p. 59).

Ideas for encouraging critical reflection

Academics play an important role in encouraging critical and reflective thinking. They can do this by asking students questions about the peer interaction process before, during and after a peer learning activity. When facilitating a group project, for example, students can be asked such questions as these:

- *Pre-activity* – What are the skills and qualities you can bring to the group? What are the biggest challenges of working in groups for you?
- *During project* – What have you and your group been doing well? What could you and you group be doing better? What will you and your group do to achieve this?
- *Post-activity* – What have you learnt about the way you work with your peers? What issues or challenges did you face when working with others? How could you do better next time?

Asking students to think about questions such as these can lead to increased self-awareness and the development of important critical thinking and reflection skills. Encouraging students to share and discuss their reflections can also lead to more effective peer learning by promoting honest communication among students and increased understanding of others. Many EAL students feel very self-conscious and anxious about what they see as their inadequate English language skills and reflective activities can encourage them to consider their strengths and weaknesses and to receive positive feedback from their peers. The importance of confidence in spoken English fluency cannot be overstressed and activities which provide EAL students with recognition of their contribution and a realisation that any errors they may make do not impede their ability to communicate are invaluable. Other ideas for encouraging critical reflection include the following.

Reflective writing tasks

Reflective writing can be a useful way of encouraging students (through assessment) to critically analyse and reflect on their learning and their assumptions, values and beliefs in relation to peer learning. In reflecting on writing assignments, students can also be asked to synthesise different perspectives they have learnt from the literature and their discussions with other students. Examples of reflective writing assignments include:

- reflective essays that require students to reflect on the group work process, including their initial assumptions and attitude to group work, their own roles within the group process and how they worked with their peers in the group project
- learning journals that require students to write frequently about their engagement in the subject, including how they interact and engage with their peers
- short reports that require students to write responses to a series of questions about their role in the group project and what they learnt from the group process.

Peer and self-assessment tasks

Increasingly, peer and self-assessment tasks are being used to assess group work, particularly group processes because these kinds of tasks encourage critical reflection and involve students more actively in the assessment process, especially if students are involved in developing the assessment criteria together with the academic. The types of peer and self-assessment tasks vary in length and complexity, from asking students to complete a checklist or itemised scoring sheet, to asking them to write reflective essays to evaluate their own as well as their peers' involvement in and contribution to the group project. These kinds of peer and self-assessment tasks require students to critically analyse and reflect on the group learning process, including how they interacted with their peers and how they incorporated and negotiated diverse perspectives and approaches to the group activity or project.

Fostering communities of learners

The ultimate goal of peer interaction across cultural groups is to foster students to collectively form a community of learners in which they share a passion for peer interaction, support each other, generate knowledge and develop a shared practice (Wenger & Snyder 2000). The sense of connectedness gives students a sense of membership and opens up communication. Students with a stronger sense of community are likely to demonstrate more efficient and effective collaborative learning outcomes and higher course satisfaction (Rovai 2002). This becomes evident when study groups decide to continue to work together at the end of a course or develop other forms of initiatives for peer learning.

Structured activities can help students to develop initiatives to continue peer interaction across cultural groups in the future. In *An Action Planning and An Action Project Assignment* (Zuniga et al. 2007), for example, participants identify three actions they are willing to take to foster peer interaction for learning across cultural groups. They partner with someone else to share their ideas, ask questions, identify the support needed to carry out these actions and create a timeline for implementation (Zuniga et al. 2007, pp. 101–2). Other ideas for fostering a community of learners are described below.

Online collaborative tools

Online tools such as discussion boards, wikis or blogs can be used to create an online community of learners. Students may, for example, be asked to respond weekly to questions or each other's posts, and their contributions may form part of an assessment task. Giving students opportunities to communicate online has numerous benefits, particularly for those who spend little time on campus because of work or family commitments. Online interaction may also be beneficial for students for whom English is a second language as they have time to formulate their responses.

Peer mentoring programs

At many higher education institutions there are various kinds of peer mentoring programs available; those that focus on subject content, such as peer-assisted study schemes, are generally semester-long programs that offer subject-specific study and revision groups. These groups are facilitated by a trained leader or mentor who is typically a high-achieving student in a senior year in the course. In most peer-assisted study schemes, the leaders or mentors are a mix of domestic and international students who support students from across different cultural and linguistic backgrounds in the subject. The established peer contact at the beginning of a semester is maintained during the semester.

Summary

The interaction for learning framework is informed by research, focuses on developing interaction within learning, teaching and assessment, and highlights the benefits of using diversity as a resource for learning. Why is this important? Increasingly, the onus is on higher education institutions to produce graduates who are work ready and have the necessary knowledge and skills to work in their professional fields. Graduates will also work with people from different cultural backgrounds so it is important that they develop skills to effectively communicate and interact. This is particularly critical for EAL students who can find that their English skills are inadequate for employment when they complete their higher education. Unless institutions provide them with ample opportunities for communication during their studies, it is all too easy for their spoken English to plateau, or even deteriorate. Ensuring that all graduates have appropriate communication skills on course completion is an important institutional objective. Where EAL students are concerned, this may require a greater level of planning within curricula than institutions are familiar with.

Academics play an important role in peer interaction with students from diverse backgrounds. Peer interaction across cultural and linguistic groups can increase students' awareness and understanding of different points of view, develop skills for a multicultural workplace and offer opportunities for international EAL students to use and develop their English language skills. The framework presented in this chapter can guide their work in this area.

CHAPTER 7

ENGLISH LANGUAGE DEVELOPMENT IN OFFSHORE EDUCATION

So far the discussion in this book has concentrated on English language development in onshore higher education courses. This chapter explores the challenges of ensuring English language standards in offshore education. The discussion is situated in the experience stage of the English language developmental continuum and highlights that within this domain, curriculum design must consider how cultural settings influence ELP development.

Over the last decade offshore education has increased dramatically and the main activity is in the Asian region. English speaking countries are the main players in offshore education, with higher education institutions from the UK, Australia and the USA involved in the delivery of programs to countries who use English as an additional or foreign language (McBurnie & Ziguras 2009).

The term 'offshore' will be used here to refer to programs that are taught in a different country from that of the awarding institution. These programs are also referred to in the literature as 'transnational' or 'cross-border education'.

Offshore programs range from branch campuses, which offer complete degrees in fully taught programs operated by a foreign higher education institution, to franchise programs, in which foreign academics teach a subject over a couple of days and the partner institution supports the students, mainly through the use of local tutors. For Australian higher education institutions, the number of students studying in offshore programs has grown from 20 000 in 1996 (McBurnie & Ziguras 2009) to 100 492 in 2009, or almost one-third of all higher education international students (Australian Education International 2011). Previous chapters have indicated the difficulty in integrating English language teaching, learning and assessment into institutional policies and practices when students are studying in an English language environment. This difficulty is exacerbated in offshore education where the tyranny of distance leads to even further challenges.

Regulation of offshore education has not highlighted English language standards in teaching, learning and assessment. This is particularly surprising given that English speaking higher education institutions are heavily and increasingly engaged in delivering offshore programs in Asia and that the region is a very culturally and linguistically diverse area, home to half the world's living languages (Marginson & McBurnie 2004).

The discussion in this chapter concentrates on degree programs delivered by Australian universities in offshore contexts in the Asia region. The reason for this is threefold. First, given that many students from Asia seek an education delivered in English, the focus of this chapter is on an English-speaking country involved in offshore teaching. Second, the use of a case study of a particular country, Australia, enables specific focus around policies and practice to be explored. Third, English-speaking countries around the world export their programs overseas and are a part of the competitive global offshore marketing community. The issues discussed here are relevant to all English-speaking universities engaged in offshore programs.

While the dominance of English in higher education is a fact (Coleman 2006), the social, historical, cultural and linguistic contexts also need be considered in order to understand the issues at stake. We do not necessarily endorse the pre-eminence of English in offshore education contexts, and recognise that the offshore higher education context is increasingly diverse and changing rapidly. Nevertheless, we accept that English programs are the dominant model, including for Australian higher education institutions (Stella & Liston 2008). As such, those students who choose to enrol in offshore programs tend to do so specifically in order to obtain a higher education qualification from an English language institution (Marginson & McBurnie 2004). Hence it is important to explore how English language can enhance or hinder the learning of students who participate in offshore programs.

Market forces have, to a large extent, driven the expansion of offshore education. As Marginson and McBurnie observe, international students and their parents appear to seek offshore education as a more affordable alternative to onshore education in gaining a degree from an English-speaking higher education institution. An English language education is usually favoured because of the growing use of English as the international language for global communication. A degree from an English-speaking institution may offer advantages in terms of employment, at home or abroad. UK, US and Australian institutions have been quick to offer offshore programs in Asia as a way of increasing their revenue; however, practice has 'run ahead of theorisation and empirical research' (Marginson 2007, p. 3). While there has been much discussion about English language standards for EAL international students in onshore programs, there has been relatively limited focus on ELP standards of offshore graduates from English-speaking higher education institutions. It is possible that the issues faced by EAL students who study onshore in English language higher education institutions are magnified in the offshore context. This places even greater importance on the way in which ELP is handled in teaching and assessment practices and raises a number of important questions about the ability of offshore EAL students to cope with their studies and graduate with appropriate skills, both in their discipline and also in English.

The Australian context

Australia has been very successful in marketing its higher education programs to international students. In 2009, international students comprised 21.5 per cent of total tertiary enrolments, the highest level for any country (OECD 2011). International student enrolments in tertiary education have remained high in 2010, and of these students 31 per cent are enrolled in distance education or offshore programs (AEI 2011). There are some concerns that onshore international student enrolments will decrease in the near future due to changes in visa requirements for graduates seeking to work in Australia after the completion of their studies. It is likely, however, that offshore enrolments will continue to rise as students seek to study at an English-speaking higher education institution in their home country.

A major concern of offshore curricula has been quality assurance (Connelly, Garton, & Olsen 2006). As the Australian Vice-Chancellors' Committee (AVCC) has argued, quality assurance mechanisms 'prove to our students, our education partners and to foreign governments that Australian education is of high quality, whether operating in Australia or overseas' (AVCC 2005, p. 3). A central concern within quality assurance is the equivalence of onshore and offshore curricula (Baird 2009; Department of Education, Science and Training 2005). It is even more complicated to ensure equivalence of English language learning outcomes between onshore and offshore curricula when it is difficult to know whether onshore students graduate with the English language skills necessary for further study or employment.

Current quality assurance measures of Australian higher education are changing in parallel with international developments such as the OECD's AHELO Feasibility Study (Coates & Richardson 2011). The major shift is from a largely fitness for purpose approach, in which quality assurance involved examining the extent to which policies and processes aligned with institutional goals, to an assurance method focused on standards, where there is a greater concentration on the agreed external measures of quality. The distinction between the two approaches can be summarised as follows.

> Whereas for fitness for purpose the key question might be: *Do policies, processes and outcomes fit the purposes of the particular higher education provider?* The questions from a standards way of thinking might be: *How do the policies and processes lead to the delivery of particular outcomes, and how do these outcomes 'measure up'?*
> (Tertiary Education Quality and Standards Agency 2011, p. 3; emphasis in original).

The shift in quality assurance purposes means that new frameworks need to be developed in order to inform quality assurance across a rapidly diversifying sector (TEQSA 2011, p. 1). For offshore curricula, the standards focus will mean that students' learning outcomes, including the English language standards of graduates in offshore programs, will be more heavily emphasised, a significant challenge for those involved in offshore education. The Tertiary Education Quality and Standards Agency is responsible for ensuring that higher education provided in Australia or by Australian providers meets the requirements of the Higher Education Standards Framework. The Higher Education Standards Framework is one element of the Australian government's new quality and regulatory arrangements for Australian higher education, which are briefly outlined below, and include developments that are currently underway within these domains (TEQSA 2010, 2011).

- *Provider standards* – minimum standards to establish the threshold that higher education providers must meet to become registered and operate as an Australian higher education provider; based on the National Protocols for Higher Education Approval Processes (MCEETYA 2007).
- *Australian Qualifications Framework* – focuses on learning outcomes and links school, vocational and higher education qualifications.
- *Information standards* – information providers should make available to prospective students to enable them to make informed decisions.
- *Teaching and learning standards* – a standards discussion paper that was developed for use in national consultation around teaching and learning standards commencing in 2011 (TEQSA 2011).
- *Research standards* – the development of benchmarks for the quality of research.

There are points of intersection between teaching and learning standards and the provider and qualifications standards (TEQSA 2011). The discussion in the teaching and learning standards paper distinguishes between teaching standards, which are defined as process or delivery standards, and learning standards, which are viewed as outcomes standards. As such, standards are not simply an outputs model of accountability; standards also need to take into consideration the processes around teaching, learning and assessment.

National standards imply a greater emphasis on agreed external reference points, which has not been the case in Australian higher education before, in either onshore or offshore curricula. Carroll and Woodhouse (2006, p. 73) state that 'It is a requirement of Australian higher education institutions offering courses abroad that the courses be "equivalent" or "comparable" to the analogous courses at home'. They acknowledge that the way this can be achieved has been largely debated within higher education in terms of what it may mean to have equivalent learning environments or the same learning outcomes. This can become more complex when ensuring levels of attainment requires onshore and offshore academic staff to develop similar understandings regarding assessment standards. Research seems to indicate that this is not always the case (Dobos 2011). Adequate English language ability is one of the main challenges that academics face in terms of maintaining standards in subjects and academic programs (Sanderson et al. 2010). English language becomes an important concern in relation to equivalence, largely because of the different linguistic and cultural contexts between onshore and offshore teaching. The current restructuring of the sector from fitness for purpose to standards will put increasing pressure on offshore curricula to ensure that their graduates have achieved equivalent learning outcomes. And in this, ELP is paramount.

Communities of practice

In order to frame the analysis of English language issues in offshore education, this section will briefly present some of the central tenets of communities of practice (Lave & Wenger 1991; Wenger 1998). We argue that offshore education essentially exports a community of practice from one country into another. In doing so several issues emerge that may need to be addressed more systematically through teaching, learning and assessment practices.

The theory of communities of practice views social practice as central to learning. Lave and Wenger (1991) refer to the process by which students are socialised into a community of practice as 'legitimate peripheral participation'. They argue that peripherality and legitimacy are required to make participation possible. Peripherality allows for opportunities for participation that give exposure to actual practice, in the sense that it 'offers the student a way of gaining access to the sources of understanding through growing involvement' (p. 37). In other words, the pedagogy becomes visible to the student when they are allowed to participate and understand the community of practice. In order to gain access to the community of practice and have the potential to become an insider, newcomers, Wenger (1998) argues, must be granted enough legitimacy to be treated as potential members. He argues that gaining legitimacy is important, as newcomers to the community 'are likely to fall short of what the community regards as competent behaviour' (p. 101). In gaining legitimacy in an English language environment, ELP is of critical importance.

One of the central notions of communities of practice is the significance of the forms of participation. Peripherality and marginality can involve both participation and non-participation. Full participation means that the student is an insider in the community of practice. Full non-participation results in being positioned as an outsider. Peripherality, where the student is exposed to actual practice but is not yet a participant, means that non-participation can lead to either full participation or the student remains on the edge of the community of practice, exposed to its practices but not a fully participating member. Despite this, learning may occur as the student is still exposed to the practices within the community but is not a fully participating member. Marginality refers to participation restricted by non-participation, where the student can be positioned as outside the community of practice or remains marginalised. According to Wenger (1998), 'Their experiences become irrelevant because they cannot be asserted and recognised as a form of competence', which negatively influences learning. Given that language is used within a community of practice to interact with others, students' ability to use the language is an important factor that contributes to gaining legitimacy within the community of practice (p. 203).

These forms of participation as developed by Lave and Wenger can be used to discuss the similarities and differences between onshore and offshore higher education communities of practice. Continuities and discontinuities across communities of practice are defined by practice, involving 'a weaving of both boundaries and peripheries' (Wenger 1998, p. 118). The boundaries and peripheries refer to the points of contact and points of difference between different communities of practice. Boundaries are defined as the aspects that distinguish between inside and outside the community, membership or non-membership of the community and inclusion or exclusion from the community. Boundaries distinguish the discontinuities between communities of practice (p. 120); peripheries enable continuities to be established between communities of practice. They refer to areas of overlap and connections with other communities of practice and to planned and unplanned opportunities for participation offered to outsiders or newcomers (p. 120). The concept of continuities and discontinuities between communities of practice is a useful framework for discussing English language in offshore education and enables an analysis to be made of some of the practices employed in this context. In particular, it will explore the peripheries that expand participation (the continuities of practice) and the boundaries that limit the possibilities of participation (the discontinuities of practice) between onshore and offshore curricula and the implications for English language.

Continuities and discontinuities of practice

Castle and Kelly (2004) propose that the main approach used by higher education institutions to achieve equivalent learning environments is to deliver the same courses to onshore and offshore students.

> The paralleling of courses on campus and offshore expedites and eases the transfer of quality assurance processes to offshore delivery. Moreover, these kinds of policies ensure transparency and accountability in practices and procedures (p. 53).

Offering the same courses in onshore and offshore contexts tends to oversimplify the process and develop barriers to teaching, learning and assessment practices within offshore education. The onshore community of practice, along with its artefacts, is transferred to another country. These artefacts include curriculum material, learning and teaching objectives, assessment tasks and learning outcomes. They contain certain assumptions about the role of English in teaching and learning in constructing understanding and in demonstrating knowledge, all of which are framed within the onshore linguistic and pedagogic framework. This community of practice is transferred to another country that has its own cultural, institutional, linguistic and historical practices that differ from those of the onshore context. Perhaps most importantly, the offshore country is one in which few, if any, students speak English as a first language. As Scarino, Crichton and Papademetre (2006) point out, simply transferring a subject from one country to another

> [e]ntails that it is possible to keep the content of a program, its accreditation, its overall curriculum design (for example, planning, teaching and learning, resourcing, assessing, evaluating) and its quality assurance 'constant', as if language and culture were neutral in this process. In this assumption there is no sense of language and culture as a medium, which mediates learning (p. 7).

This approach adopts a one size fits all approach to offshore education. It assumes a neutral context, and does not necessarily take into account the local contexts of the students (Widdowson 2004) including their mother tongue. So boundaries are developed in which challenges emerge for the inclusion of the local linguistic and cultural context in planning offshore curricula. This has implications for academics and students in terms of their participation and positioning within the offshore community of practice.

In Australia, the International Education Association of Australia (IEAA 2008) developed a good practice guide for Australian institutions engaged in offshore delivery. It found that there were several critical success factors for teaching and learning in offshore programs. These included the following.

- Australian academics and managers need to know the educational and cultural context offshore.
- Educational programs must be contextualised for offshore delivery.
- Internationalising the curriculum can support contextualisation of programs.
- Internationalisation and contextualisation should be done with local offshore input.
- All staff must have intercultural skills, teaching experience and appropriate qualifications.

- Academics need to be able to develop students' English language skills.
- Learning outcomes and assessment of student learning must be equivalent to comparable onshore programs.
- Academic entry standards must be equivalent to comparable onshore programs and must pay attention to students' English language proficiency.
- Information, communication and educational technologies should be used to support student learning.
- Students should have appropriate access to learning resources and services.
- Offshore programs should routinely employ a range of evaluation strategies and act on findings (p. 72).

Included in the success factors are issues about students' English language skills. These relate to ensuring that entry standards are comparable to onshore programs, that academics develop students' English language skills during their study period and that assessment is equivalent to onshore curricula. Yet there are very few studies that have explored the ways in which the different aspects are implemented in offshore education.

While there is little research on English language and offshore students, the many studies investigating issues related to English language and onshore international EAL students can be drawn on to indicate issues that may emerge in the offshore context. Most of these studies have highlighted the isolation that some international EAL students feel, in part due to their perceptions of their English language competence. These range from difficulties participating in the academic culture due to their perceived lack of English language skills (Carroll 2005), to extra time pressures created by studying in English (O'Loughlin & Arkoudis 2009; Prescott & Hellstén 2005) and difficulties accommodating the dominant conventions of academic writing in English-medium institutions (Basturkmen & Lewis 2002; Ferguson 1997; Fox 1994; Phan 1999, 2001). Along with issues of English language skills, international students also encounter challenges in acculturating into the academic discourse community of their field of study (Arkoudis & Tran 2010; Carroll 2005; Koehne 2005; Morita 2004). It would appear that disciplinary communities of practice and international students' perceptions of their competence and, therefore, their belonging are relevant issues for onshore students and important to consider as possible sites for continuities and discontinuities of practice in offshore education.

The role of language in content teaching

In onshore teaching, the academic structures the learning environment through the use of English. This is evidenced by how the language is used to convey the content, by the teaching and learning approaches that are used to discuss and develop the students' disciplinary knowledge and by the language requirements of the assessment tasks. The students, who have limited exposure to academic English, do not absorb the required disciplinary discourse by osmosis. The fact that in most offshore contexts English is learnt as an additional language means that some students' access or ability to use English in the learning community may place them as outsiders or as marginal to the community of practice.

Transporting curricula from onshore to offshore contexts means that the content knowledge is in English. Students may find it difficult to understand the material and become overwhelmed with what they are required to learn (Chapman & Pyvis 2009). One solution to help bridge the gap is to encourage students to use their first language to enhance their understanding of abstract concepts. Students would be encouraged to seek parallel sources and material in their first language, work with peers, brainstorm ideas with their common language and keep notes in the dominant language to ease the pressure. This would create continuities between the students' and the academics' community of practice by (re)positioning the students' linguistic background as an important learning tool within the learning community.

Living outside an English-speaking community, offshore EAL students are not likely to have the same exposure to the English language as their onshore counterparts. They may be able to access the internet and a variety of television programs in English, but many have few opportunities to interact with those who have English as a first language. The reality in offshore education is that EAL students will need to develop their English language skills while completing their degree; using only English to teach the content can have negative consequences for learning. As was discussed in previous chapters, students' English development in onshore curricula is not necessarily integrated into subject teaching and assessment – but this would need to be the case in offshore curricula, due in part to the different local context within which learning in taking place. In order to ensure continuities of practice between onshore and offshore curricula, English language development may need to be incorporated into disciplinary teaching, learning and assessment practices. If it were, this would ensure equivalence in learning outcomes between offshore and onshore students.

Teaching and learning approaches

A further concern is that academics' use of the specific disciplinary discourse and the epistemology that guides their teaching in the onshore context may not be appropriate for the offshore teaching context. Leask (2004) maintains that there is a difference between teaching international students in an Australian higher education institution and teaching students in their home country. In the students' home country the academic is a 'cultural outsider in the offshore location' (p. 2). The offshore students share common experiences of the education system in their home country, teaching and learning approaches used by their academics, notions of how to be successful in their academic work and a localised used of English that constructs their local identities and values (Observatory on Borderless Higher Education 2007). These background experiences frame their understanding of the community of practice they are entering. Attempting to reproduce an equivalent learning environment to the onshore program could limit students' participation in the community of practice. The students, who may be struggling to understand what is expected of them in terms of participation, may also experience difficulties with using English to participate in the learning community, which could result in them not participating in the teaching and learning activities, further positioning them as outsiders. The learning environment would be linguistically and culturally different from students' previous experiences; this can create discontinuities of practice.

English language support services in higher education institutions' offshore campuses are structured in similar ways to the onshore language support services (Stella & Liston 2008). Students seek out these services for assistance and guidance with completing written assessment. As Stella and Liston (2008, p. 45) point out, English language skills are a 'cause of tension among some staff and students'; they suggest attempting to address this tension through increased web-based resources and additional English language support programs. This approach may need to be accompanied by English language teaching that is discipline-specific and that develops the language skills necessary for completing assessment tasks.

We know anecdotally and from research in onshore contexts that academics find it very difficult to address the language and learning needs of international EAL students. In onshore teaching, academics perceive their responsibility as teaching the content of their subject area, and view English language as the responsibility of students. English language development is largely considered an add-on to disciplinary learning and teaching. The need to embed English language teaching in disciplinary teaching and learning in offshore programs is even more pressing, the reason being that many offshore curricula have lower English language entry requirements than EAL international students studying in onshore curricula. To deal with this, offshore English language teaching should be conceptualised as integral to achieving disciplinary learning outcomes and not be treated in the same way as onshore curricula. This reconsideration may require embedding English language within disciplinary teaching and learning. If this were to occur, English language would be incorporated into curriculum design, which would include disciplinary content, teaching and learning approaches and assessment. In order to create continuities of practice between onshore and offshore programs, English language development needs to be included within teaching and learning practices alongside English language support programs and web-based resources.

Assessment

Assessment defines the curriculum and student learning. James et al. (2002) have pointed out that

> For most students, assessment requirements literally define the curriculum. Assessment is a potent strategic tool for educators with which to spell out the learning that will be rewarded and to guide students into effective approaches to study (p. 1).

If English is to be part of the taught curriculum in offshore programs and if English language development is important to achieving learning outcomes, then it should also be included in the assessment for subjects. The assessment criterion would be measuring the extent to which students in the subject, regardless of where it was taught, have achieved a satisfactory result. In other words, it is through the assessment that equivalence between offshore and onshore curricula can be measured, in particular the English language levels of student attainment, and thus enhance continuities of practice.

Moderation between onshore and offshore staff would be required to ensure that there is comparability across assessment practices. Sanderson et al. (2010) have developed a toolkit that can be used for moderation of assessment between onshore and offshore academics. They have found that the communication between staff is important and have included a checklist of good practice in moderation of assessment. This checklist must also include moderation around English language, such as

- assignment of English language learning outcomes for the subject
- development of marking criteria that include English language oral and/or written communication
- discussion of any variations and different interpretations of English language skills in assessment of students' work
- marking a selection of assignments and discussion of how marks were assigned
- development of English language assessment expertise through professional development.

Any moderation meeting must include the English language specialists who will guide the English language assessment practices of academics. They can guide discussion and, through varied interactions, shared understandings of English language assessment can be developed between onshore, offshore and English language specialists, thereby increasing the continuities of practice across the different learning sites.

English language development in offshore education

Practical strategies for offshore ELP curriculum design

Figure 7.1 aims to capture the different aspects of developing offshore curricula in terms of English language issues discussed above.

This diagram represents the interrelated nature of curriculum design. At the centre of the circles are the learning outcomes. Here, the focus is on what the students should be able to demonstrate by the end of the subject. The objectives and learning outcomes could be similar to those of the onshore curricula, thereby maintaining continuity between the two learning sites. How those outcomes are achieved may vary between the onshore and offshore teaching environment. The three circles represent the content of the subject, the teaching and learning approaches used by the academic and the assessment of the subject. The overlaps between the circles represents the shifts and changes that need to be made for teaching in the offshore context in order to achieve equivalent outcomes and establish continuities of practice between the two teaching sites.

Each of these overlapping areas will be discussed with regard to issues that may be considered in planning offshore teaching. The focus will be on achieving equivalence of outcome in the depth and quality of offshore teaching through selection of content, adapting teaching and learning approaches and matters involving assessment tasks. More specifically, Table 7.1 draws on the discontinuities of practice that were identified in the above discussion.

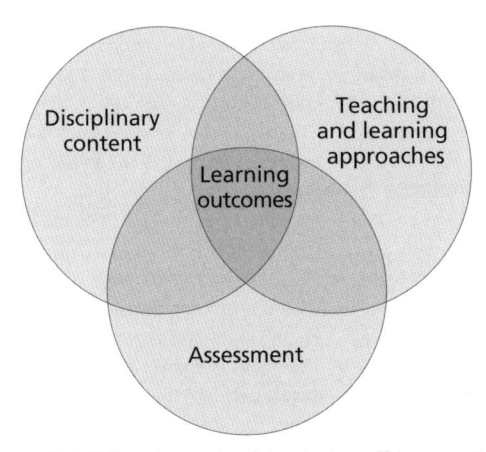

Figure 7.1: Different aspects of developing offshore curricula

Table 7.1: Continuities of practice in onshore and offshore curricula

Onshore	Offshore
Content: Language used to communicate concepts	
• Course material and delivery in English only. • English language construction of knowledge and discourses used within the discipline. • Examples and case studies relevant to onshore contexts and/or professional accreditation.	• Course material may include material in students' first language to support their understanding of the concepts. • Highlight the differences between the construction of knowledge in English and students' first language. • Localise the examples and case studies to increase relevance to students' context and/or professional accreditation. • The above examples emphasise the importance of working closely with local academic staff.
Teaching and learning: Language used to enhance learning	
• English the only language of communication. • Monocultural Western approaches adopted for teaching and learning. • Approaches adopted are usually located within the communities of practice of the discipline. • Students are offered English language support programs.	• Decisions will need to be made about when first language can be used to facilitate learning and when English will be used. • Supporting students' learning by focusing on how English language is used to express ideas. • Model practices of critical thinking as they relate to the students' cultural background and highlight the similarities and differences when using English. • Adopting local approaches to teaching and learning. • First language can assist students in their learning. • The above examples emphasise adopting local approaches to enhance student learning.
Assessment: Language used to demonstrate understandings	
• Developed by academic staff to assess the students' understanding with reference to the objectives and learning outcomes. • Criteria are developed that assess the level of understanding with reference to the materials and contexts discussed in class. • Depending on the discipline, English language skills can be included in the criteria sheet.	• Collaborate with bilingual academic staff in designing assessment tasks to ensure that they are culturally and linguistically unambiguous. • Criteria developed that assess the level of understanding, with reference to the materials and contexts discussed in class. • English language skills to be included in the criteria sheet. • Moderation of assessment to assist in developing shared understandings regarding assessment of English language learning outcomes. • The above examples involve collaboration with local academics to ensure that assessment tasks are linguistically and culturally appropriate, while also achieving the learning outcomes of the subject.

English language development in offshore education

Table 7.1 attempts to embed the cultural and linguistic considerations in designing curricula for offshore education. It is not a complete list, but rather one that can be added to as academics draw on their own experiences of offshore education and their disciplinary background. It highlights three important aspects arising from English language in offshore contexts. First, that the use of students' first language is a very useful source that can help enhance student learning. As EAL students are usually more competent in their first language, it would be important to develop strategies that draw on the linguistic resources that the students bring to the learning task. Second, that the English language discourse used within the discipline should be emphasised. If students are to participate and feel included in the community of practice, then it is important that the English language used to construct disciplinary knowledge is taught in offshore curricula. Third, that it is important to collaborate with local academics working in the program. They can assist in developing material, teaching and learning and assessment tasks that are linguistically and culturally appropriate for the students.

Summary

This chapter has explored some of the issues relating to developing ELP within offshore curricula. There has been a huge investment in offshore education by importers and exporters of these programs, mainly driven by market forces. English-speaking higher education institutions have been quick to develop programs to meet the ever-growing demand from the Asia–Pacific region. Yet at a policy level there is much debate about what equivalence may mean in offshore teaching; most of these policies neglect English language development within disciplinary curricula and assessment practices. We have argued that transferring programs from one country to another can create discontinuities of practice which do not necessarily ensure English language standards between onshore and offshore graduates. Boundaries around the offshore community of practice emerge when the local linguistic and cultural contexts are not taken into consideration in the planning and delivery of the subject. These include the use of English to communicate content, teaching and learning approaches, and assessment tasks that are constructed within a Western cultural and linguistic framework. Central to participating in the community of practice is the use of language to express knowledge, demonstrate understanding and explore areas of uncertainty. If Anglo constructs of language and learning dominate the community of practice, offshore students may be marginalised or positioned outside the community of practice. This can hinder student learning.

Such discontinuities of practice lead to a consideration of teaching practice within offshore education, which could be more sensitive to students' linguistic and cultural backgrounds. Within communities of practice, participation is central to students gaining access to the learning environment and becoming competent members of the community. In most offshore contexts, English is taught as a foreign language and students do not have the same exposure to English as they may have onshore in an English-speaking environment. Curriculum design for offshore programs should incorporate both English language and content teaching. Careful attention needs to be paid to the linguistic and cultural assumptions that underpin the content taught, the teaching and learning approaches adopted and the assessment tasks employed. Extra attention to these could result in enhanced student learning, the achievement of depth and quality in offshore education and equivalence in outcomes with onshore curricula.

CHAPTER 8

ENGLISH LANGUAGE PROFICIENCY AND WORKPLACE READINESS

The previous chapters have emphasised the important role of English language proficiency for academic studies and argued that English language outcomes should be incorporated within disciplinary curriculum design and assessment practices. Thus far we have addressed the 'entry' and 'experience' stages of the ELP development continuum. This chapter turns to the final stage in the continuum — 'exit'. We do so by examining the influence of English language proficiency in the workplace readiness and employment outcomes of graduates with English as an additional language. The importance of ELP for workplace readiness and employment outcomes is well known, with English language ability recognised as being extremely influential in determining employment outcomes. Increasingly, the argument has been made that professionals cannot take their place in a knowledge economy if they lack sophisticated spoken and written English skills. Within professions such as medicine, nursing, teaching, accountancy and engineering, high level English ability is increasingly considered to be essential by employers and professional associations around the world.

Australian higher education institutions, for the most part, acknowledge the importance of graduates' ELP – often expressed as generic communication skills – in their statement of graduate attributes. In recent years, however, questions have been raised about the role and effectiveness of institutions in producing highly employable, skilled graduates and there has been growing media attention on the poor workplace readiness employment outcomes of

EAL graduates (Maley 2008; O'Keefe 2006). These concerns have also been raised in the UK where there have been a number of news articles questioning the English language proficiency of international students studying in the UK and criticisms that students graduate without adequate English communication skills (Coughlan 2008; Newman 2008). The common question asked is: What use is a degree if students can't function in a workplace? This chapter discusses the graduate skills and attributes sought by employers and examines the influence of ELP on the workplace readiness and employment outcomes of EAL students.

What are employers looking for in graduates with English as an additional language?

In the past decade numerous studies have examined the graduate skills and attributes sought by the professions. In Baik's (2010) study of academics' assessment practices, academics teaching in professional degrees emphasised the importance of professional communication. Examples of these views are encapsulated in the following two quotes.

> One of the major issues in the various professions we send students to, is they require students who are communicators, written in particular.
>
> Academic, Engineering

> I think it is a professional qualification as well as an academic qualification, and as members of the profession, graduates have to be able to communicate.
>
> Academic, Law

Research on this topic clearly shows that employers place high importance on English language communication skills. In a large national survey of 271 employers, conducted in Australia in 2006, communication skills were rated far higher than other items, including qualifications and previous employment, as the most important selection criteria when hiring graduates (see Table 6.1)

(Graduate Careers Australia 2008). Although communication skills are listed separately to cultural or social fit, teamwork skills, and reasoning and analytical skills, we argue that these skills fall under the broader category of ELP. The literature on second language acquisition has emphasised the importance of language use in context, meaning that appropriate register, negotiating with colleagues, use of humour and ability to interact informally with others are important in demonstrating proficiency in a language. These skills cannot be easily isolated because they all require the use of English language in different contexts. If they are grouped together, then clearly English language proficiency is an important issue for all graduating students.

This is consistent with other research that highlights the importance placed on communication skills in the professions. Employer perspectives on the importance of ELP in the workplace were explored by Arkoudis et al. (2009) in their study of the impact of English language proficiency and workplace readiness on the employment outcomes and performance of tertiary international students. Among the interview participants were 36 employers and members of Australia-wide regulatory bodies from the health, engineering, accounting and information technology professions. A strong theme to emerge from the interview data was the importance of ELP. In all the professions reading, writing, speaking and listening were considered vital. More important than high academic achievement was a graduate's broader set of skills and attributes, the whole package, including the ability to work in teams and get along in a small group. This necessarily means having a high level of ELP, socially and professionally.

Table 8.1: Most important skills and attributes required of recruiting graduates

Skills and attributes	As ranked by employers
Communication skills (written and oral)	1
Reasoning and analytical or technical skills	2
Attitude, drive and commitment	3
Cultural and social alignment and values fit	4
Academic qualifications	5
Teamwork skills	6
Emotional intelligence	7
Work experience	8
Intra and extracurricular activities	9
Leadership skills	10

Source: Graduate Careers Australia 2008

English language proficiency is a high-stakes issue for graduate job access. From the start of the recruitment process, candidates' written applications are systematically sifted before the next interview stage in which spoken communication skills become essential. Within the engineering field, for example, researchers have shown that effective communication skills are considered to be vital, in particular, graduates' capacity for organisational 'verbal interaction' (Hawthorne 1994). Similarly in the accounting field, Watty's study (2007) highlighted the priority placed on effective communication skills. She reported that while employers were satisfied with the technical competence of graduates, they often recruited graduates from fields other than accounting due to the need for employees with effective communication skills.

In addition to the oral communication skills necessary for day to day work, many of the employers across professional fields in Arkoudis et al.'s study (2009) mentioned the importance of high-level writing skills for written reports that were frequently required in various professions. Employers were critical of the level of writing skills they were often presented with in the workplace.

These findings are consistent with a more recent national survey of Australian employers in 338 companies across Australia. The findings highlight employers' concerns about the workplace readiness of graduates, particularly in relation to communication skills. The large majority (75 per cent) of the employers reported that their business suffered because of poor literacy skills and that workers, even those with adequate literacy levels, were unable to perform some workplace communication tasks at the required standard (Australian Industry Group 2010).

Testing of English language proficiency for employment purposes

The growing concern about the ELP of graduates has led to the use of English language testing by employers. Internationally benchmarked tests such as IELTS and TOEFL are used to indicate graduates' English language ability. As well as these international tests, there are also nationally based tests such as the Occupational English Test (OET), which is designed to test language proficiency for the health professions. The data on the IELTS website (2008) show that the frequency distribution by reasons for taking an IELTS test for 2007 were slightly higher for entry to employment compared to entry for higher education courses, revealing the growing trend of using IELTS for employment purposes. According to Merrifield (2008, p. 268), IELTS is increasingly being used for 'purposes of language assessment for immigration and entry to professions'.

In the last four years employer groups in Australia have increasingly indicated their own minimum English language requirements for graduates seeking employment in Australia. Accountancy firm KPMG, for example, has introduced as a requirement an IELTS score of 7.0 for job applicants; Ernst & Young's requirement is for an IELTS overall band score of 7.5. Possession of an IELTS overall band score 7 (or equivalent) is now mandatory for practice in all Australian clinically based professions, including for conditionally registered international students while in training. Since July 2005 Australian state and territory medical registration boards have also expanded mandatory testing to include temporary as well as permanent resident international medical graduates. In addition, in 2010 the newly formed Nursing and Midwifery Board raised its minimum English language standards to IELTS 7.0 in each of the four components, thereby denying many international EAL student nurses registration, a possible result of which was hundreds of international student nurses facing deportation after graduation, despite the well-known national shortage of nurses (Trouson 2010).

Clearly, the increasing use of IELTS by employers to set minimum ELP requirements is a response to ongoing concerns about the communication skills of international EAL students. The notion of international students taking an IELTS exit test on completion of their studies has been suggested by IDP (Healy 2008) and is supported by several Australian higher education institutions, which offer IELTS testing for graduates in order to support their efforts to find employment. There has been some criticism from language experts about the validity of using such tests for purposes other than entry into higher education. O'Loughlin (2008 p. 78), for example, writes that

> Despite being developed solely as university selection tests of academic English, the IELTS and the TOEFL have recently been employed for the accreditation of health professionals and also

proposed as university exit tests without any serious attempt to validate them for either purpose. The uses of both tests are therefore considered by many language-testing specialists to be unethical.

The increased use by employers of a language test such as IELTS and the recent media focus on the ELP of international graduates may suggest that ELP is the only, or most important, factor affecting EAL graduates' workplace readiness. Evidence suggests that factors other than ELP can also influence EAL students' employment outcomes, however. Even when EAL students have achieved adequate English language levels for employment, they may still face difficulties securing work in their chosen field. Indeed, numerous studies have shown that EAL international students face more challenges and difficulties in finding work in a field related to their studies and that their employment outcomes are far poorer than those of their domestic counterparts. The following section examines recent published studies on EAL students' employment outcomes.

Employment outcomes of students with English as an additional language

As outlined in the introductory chapter to this book, the international higher education market is highly competitive, with fierce competition among higher education institutions to attract fee-paying international students. Recent times, however, have seen the emergence of a new rationale for international student education: competition for skilled labour (de Witt 2008). Many countries are experiencing ageing populations alongside pressure to compete in the global knowledge economy. Industrial societies such as Europe, North America, Japan and Australia are competing for talented students to fill their skill needs. Within these societies there are particular needs in specific skilled employment areas that governments are attempting to address through immigration policies. The implication of this for education in Australia is that the focus has shifted from international students returning to their home country after their studies to retaining international students

English language proficiency and workplace readiness

who can apply for permanent residency and fill the skills needs that exist in the country.

The opportunity to work in a host country after graduation is becoming a common marketing tool for countries competing in the international education market (Hawthorne 2009; Lasanowski & Verbik 2007). While most students return to their countries of origin after completing their studies, a large proportion seek to remain in their host countries. This is a trend observed in industrial countries such as Australia, the UK, Canada and Japan. As more students seek to remain in their host countries and find employment, ELP has been placed under the spotlight as an important factor in influencing workplace readiness and employment outcomes of these graduates.

In 2004 and 2006, Australian Education International (AEI) conducted two large-scale national surveys on the perceptions and experiences of international students. The findings of both surveys indicate that international EAL students do indeed face more difficulties finding employment in Australia than do domestic graduates for whom English is a first language (AEI 2007b, 2008). Just over half of the international students surveyed in 2006 intended to find a job after graduation, yet only 38 per cent of those responding to the follow-up survey had found a job immediately after their studies, while 17 per cent were still looking for a job. Domestic students were more successful in finding a job: 48 per cent had intended to find a job after graduation and 40 per cent managed to do so. Among international students, the most successful in finding employment were those from Europe (51 per cent), the least successful those from southern and central Asia (22 per cent). Those international students who did find work in Australia reported that it was very difficult or somewhat difficult to do so (33 per cent). Those most likely to report difficulties in finding work were also students from southern and central Asia (44 per cent). These findings supported those of other studies, such as the 2006 skilled immigration review (Birrell, Hawthorne, & Richardson 2006) and are borne out in longitudinal research (AEI 2007a).

Birrell and Healy (2008) conclude that language deficiencies are a major factor in explaining different employment outcomes between domestic and international graduates. They argue that immigrants trained overseas have better chances of getting a job in

Australia than international students who undertook their education here, a finding that suggests that the English language advantage bestowed by Australian training is outweighed by the professional experience accumulated by older immigrants who trained overseas. The authors found that international students from EAL countries are less successful at finding professional or managerial employment (22 per cent) than are those who also come from non-English-speaking countries but who undertook their education or training overseas (36 per cent). Even in accounting, where there is a strong employer demand, Australian-trained international students were the least successful group in finding professional employment. This suggests that work experience, alongside recent training, is an important factor.

This interpretation is supported by an AEI study (2007a) that indicated that the main difficulties faced by international students in finding jobs included lack of work experience and permanent resident status, inability to find employment in their field of interest, English language barriers and an implication that employers prefer domestic to international graduates In a later study (2010), AEI found that 73 per cent of international students who had completed a higher education degree were working in their field of study. This was a higher level than in the earlier surveys. Of those who were unemployed or looking for work, lack of work experience, not having permanent residency and a lack of jobs in the graduate's field of study were considered to be the obstacles to employment. It can be concluded that no one single factor is the key barrier to employment, indicating that perhaps there are factors other than ELP that influence successful employment outcomes.

When considering the difficulties EAL graduates from diverse cultural backgrounds may face in integrating into their new communities, it is evident that such challenges would be further compounded in a workplace, and even more so in the stressful situation of a job interview. This has implications for higher education institutions to provide English language programs that meet not only the student's academic needs, but also prepare them for the workplace. To date, programs taking such an integrated approach have been limited. Most English language programs offered in higher education institutions involve the development of academic literacy skills. While these skills are important for the achievement in students' academic courses, research has also pointed to social communicative skills as being important, especially in the context of developing skills for employment (Duff 2008; O'Loughlin & Arkoudis 2009). It is fair to say that most of the research on English language development in higher education institutions has largely ignored any links between English language development, study and employment (Hawthorne 2007).

Watty's (2007) study was one of the few to link language learning during tertiary study with employment outcomes. This author highlights some of the concerns that emerge concerning the alignment between English language development and employer expectations, and notes the reluctance of higher education institutions to insist on additional class requirements for EAL students due to fear of jeopardising their market position in the competitive and lucrative area of international education. For academic staff involved in teaching international students, there are tensions between teaching content that is seen as directly relevant to the students' future employment and the communication skills that the students also need for employment but which are not necessarily taught within the course of study.

The published research discussed above shows that international EAL graduates have relatively poor employment outcomes in comparison with their peers. While there is considerable research on employers' perspectives of ELP and workplace readiness, we know very little about students' perceptions and experiences in finding work in their field of study. The following section discusses recent research that examines workplace readiness from the EAL students' perspective, specifically, the extent to which English language proficiency influences workplace readiness and employment outcomes for international students seeking employment in English-speaking environments.

Workplace readiness

As has already been discussed in this book, student expectations and perceptions are critical to their motivation to develop ELP while at a higher education institution. If ELP is considered to be unimportant for academic achievement or successful employment outcomes, students are less like to devote energy and time to develop their ELP. What are student perceptions about the skills sought after by employers? In Table 8.2 (below), we have taken the employer perspectives shown in Table 8.1 and added a column showing the graduates' perspectives. The table shows that students, like employers, place high importance on communication skills and less relative importance on extracurricular activities and work experience. There are, however, some areas of mismatch between the skills graduates consider to be valued by employers and the skills employers themselves value. The biggest difference can be seen in their beliefs about how employers value 'cultural/social fit'. Whereas employers placed a relatively high importance on this attribute (ranking it at number four), students did not see this as being as important, ranking it in ninth place.

Similar findings were uncovered in the AEI (2010) survey concerning the different perceptions of the importance of communication skills from graduates and employers. It is important to point out that the findings reported in Table 8.2 were from a survey administered to international and domestic higher education students across Australia. We do not know whether EAL students, specifically international EAL, have different views to their peers. To gain more insight into the perceptions and experiences of international EAL students and graduates, the next section reports on a study that investigated the key factors that influenced international EAL students' workplace readiness and employment outcomes. Specifically, the project aimed to examine the influence of ELP on workplace readiness and the extent to which factors (other than ELP) influenced employment outcomes.

Table 8.2: Importance of skills and personal attributes to graduate recruiters and students

Skills and attributes	As ranked by employers	As ranked by students
Communication skills (written and oral)	1	2
Reasoning and analytical or technical skills	2	4
Attitude, drive and commitment	3	1
Cultural or social alignment and values fit	4	9
Academic qualifications	5	7
Teamwork skills	6	3
Emotional intelligence	7	5
Work experience	8	8
Intra and extracurricular activities	9	10
Leadership skills	10	6

Source: Graduate Careers Australia 2008

An Australian study of workplace readiness and employment outcomes

The study, supported by the Commonwealth Department of Education, Employment and Workplace Relations (DEEWR), was undertaken in 2008–09 by a team of researchers, including two of the authors of this book (Arkoudis et al. 2009). Central to the study was the relationship between ELP and workplace readiness to achieve successful employment outcomes. This was defined within the project as graduates finding employment in their qualified field of study or a comparable area relating to their qualifications. Unsuccessful outcomes were defined as employment in a lower-level field not related to their qualification or training, underemployment or unemployment. The term 'domestic students/graduates' was used to refer to Australian students and graduates (typically, permanent residents or Australian citizens) who had completed most or all of their education in Australia and who speak English as their first language. Recent graduates were defined as those who completed tertiary degrees in Australia in the past two years.

The study reported in this chapter was part of a larger study involving a detailed review of relevant literature, semi-structured interviews, focus groups and analyses of three statistical data sets – Australian 2006 Census data, Australian Education International data from 2002 to 2008 and the 2006 Longitudinal Survey on Immigrants to Australia. The study explored international and domestic students and graduates' perceptions about the factors affecting workplace readiness and employment outcomes, including the role and importance of ELP. In addition, the study aimed to gain insight into the experiences of recent graduates in finding work in their chosen field of study. The study involved semi-structured interviews with final year students and recent graduates. Interviewees were 40 international EAL final year students and recent graduates, and 18 domestic students and recent graduates for whom English was the first language. In total, 58 students or graduates from various language backgrounds and fields of study participated in the study. The final year students were recruited from two Australian tertiary institutions with diverse student cohorts. Most of the international students had been studying in Australia for between one and four years, with the exception of three students who had been in Australia for more than six years.

In addition to the students and graduates, interviews were conducted with higher education staff from 10 institutions. Staff included employment and career officers, leaders of academic language and learning units and disciplinary academic staff involved in teaching in professional courses.

Employment aspirations and experiences of students with English as an additional language

Consistent with the national survey data discussed above, most international EAL students in the Arkoudis et al. study indicated that they hoped to work in Australia after completing their courses, and most planned to find work in their chosen field of study. Although many stated that their ELP would need ongoing development if they hoped to be promoted to a management position, they generally believed that their ELP and profession-related skills were adequate for an entry level position in their chosen field. Many had actively sought assistance in preparing their résumés and job applications from higher education institutions' career centres and faculty staff. Despite their aspirations to remain in Australia and work in their chosen field, all the final year international students, regardless of discipline, expressed difficulty in finding work in their chosen field. Of 20 final year international students interviewed, only four medical students had secured full-time positions for the following year (2009). Most of the other students indicated that they had already started to apply for full-time positions in their field of study.

Recent graduates were also included and they, too, expressed difficulty in finding work. Fewer than half of the international recent graduates had found full-time positions in their chosen field. A few graduates had found part-time work in their chosen field but had to supplement their income by working in restaurants or shops. Most of the graduates mentioned that they had not even been successful in reaching the interview stage. Others had found work in areas unrelated to their studies, mainly in the hospitality or retail industries.

English language proficiency and workplace readiness

When international graduates were asked about the possible reasons for the difficulty experienced in finding work, two key factors clearly emerged: inadequate English language proficiency and lack of prior work experience. Ben's case is a common story among international student graduates.

CASE STUDY 8.1: GRADUATE EXPERIENCE OF HIRING PROCESSES

Ben has been in Australia for almost four years, during which time he has completed an accounting degree. For the past year, he has been working as a part-time accountant in a small company run by Chinese-speaking employers. To supplement his income, he also works as a waiter in a Chinese restaurant. According to Ben, he has applied for 'hundreds, maybe a thousand' full-time accounting positions but has been unsuccessful each time. He believes that his higher education course prepared him extremely well for the workplace and that he has the necessary language skills to perform well in an entry-level accounting position, but for some reason, he says, 'They really don't want to hire us.'

Ben believes that international graduates are disadvantaged by the hiring process, especially when potential employers call applicants by telephone before arranging a face-to-face interview. For Ben, whose first language is Chinese, communicating on the telephone (without the cues from body language) is far more difficult than talking face to face. He notes: 'There is very little choice to get interview, they just call me and say, hello, and [speak] very quickly and maybe if you say, "pardon" or "sorry", they will think, oh, you are not good communicator.'

Ben has a number of Chinese friends who also graduated with Australian accounting degrees, but after six months have given up applying for positions in their field of study. They are mostly working in the restaurant industry now.

Despite the numerous rejections and setbacks he has faced, Ben plans to continue applying for full-time positions in accounting. He is also exploring options for further postgraduate studies in commerce.

Ben and many other EAL graduates' experience in the study is in stark contrast to the experience of the domestic graduates, all of whom (except one pursuing an academic career) had found full-time work in positions directly related to their field of study. In addition, half the domestic final year students had secured full-time graduate positions for the following year. The other five students had not begun actively seeking graduate positions as they still had one to two semesters remaining in their degrees. All of them felt confident that they would be able to find work in their chosen field before graduating from their course.

How important is English language proficiency in finding work?

The findings from the Arkoudis et al. study reveal a major difference in domestic and international EAL students' perceptions. International students and graduates agreed that ELP was very important for finding work in their chosen field. Specifically, they felt that communication skills in the job interview were essential, as were the skills to interact with co-workers and clients. The issue of accent (and employers' perceptions of graduates with different accents) was raised as a potential obstacle to gaining work in their chosen field. Domestic students focused less on ELP, although they recognised the importance of communication skills for the workplace. Just over one-half of them believed that ELP was essential; a few thought it was not important for finding work in their field of study.

The job interview

Almost all the international students and graduates thought that ELP, especially speaking proficiency, was essential for finding work, particularly for the job interview. They recognised the importance of ELP in impression created and in competitive advantage (or disadvantage). A number of students stated that ELP was the most important factor for success in job applications: ELP not only affected one's ability to communicate, but it affected their confidence and hence performance in interviews. This view is captured by the following quote:

> I think if I want to rank the elements that would help you to find a job I would rank English first ... I think English is important in two ways. The first one is to make you more confident when you are in the interview or when you were, when you started your

English language proficiency and workplace readiness

job. Another thing is of course the employers would compare, you know, the applicants based on English language skills.

Chinese student, Commerce

Although most international students and graduates believed ELP to be very important for gaining work in their chosen field, some interviewees indicated that the importance of English language skills depended upon the type of work one was doing. For example, in some areas of work in information technology and engineering, technical skills and knowledge were considered far more important and thus sought after by employers. English language skills were not considered to be very important in these fields.

Job performance

Whereas not all interviewees agreed that ELP was crucial for finding work in their chosen field, they all agreed ELP was essential for performing well in the workplace, particularly for promotion to more senior positions. A number of interviewees deemed ELP, or 'communication skills', to be the most important factor in performing well in the workplace. This is related to not just technical language but 'small talk' and casual conversation. While a few EAL graduates, particularly those in information technology fields, thought that ELP would not be important for job performance, others referred to the importance of ELP for social interaction even if a high level was not required to carry out the work.

In addition to job performance, a high level of ELP was seen as being essential for promotion. Most international students and graduates believed that their chances of promotion or career advancement would be limited because of their level of ELP. In fact, limited opportunities for promotion or advancement was one of the reasons given for graduates moving outside their field of study, as reflected in the following quote.

> I know most of the students doing accounting, they want to get a job in accounting area and because in this area it is very hard to be promoted and salary and the pay no good, so ... many of my friends that have been after three or five or after several years they would like to consider to changing to other areas.

Chinese student, Accounting

145

English Language Standards in Higher Education

This view is supported by employers and regulatory bodies interviewed for another part of the study (Arkoudis et al. 2009). The employers indicated that poor ELP increased the risk of international student graduates' career stagnation and perhaps ultimate dismissal.

Domestic students and graduates also saw the importance of having complex English language skills. In terms of performing well in the job, one domestic higher education graduate, currently working as an engineer, commented on the importance of being able to adapt language use to suit the specific context. This requires quite sophisticated knowledge and control of the English language. In particular, he mentioned the importance of having an understanding and control of register.

> Absolutely [important] in a project office ... there's a lot of the typical construction guys who are walking around and just sort of swearing and grunt a lot and then at the same time I deal with a lot of the professional, the public, the very professional people ... and I have to, the language I use with dealing with those different people changes, abruptly ... Like, I'll have a conversation with someone where we're both swearing and then next time, then I'm on the phone to someone being very polite.
>
> Domestic graduate, Engineering

Being able to switch registers appropriately requires not only linguistic, but also cultural understanding, which is related to the attribute valued by employers mentioned earlier, that is, 'cultural/social fit'.

Social interaction and cultural fit

The importance of being able to understand and adapt to Australian work culture was raised by a number of interviewees – both domestic and international. One domestic graduate thought that employers' perception of a graduate's cultural fit was a factor influencing employment outcomes. A number of other interviewees also commented on the importance of being able to understand the cultural meanings behind the language.

> I think even if an international student might be brilliant at doing accounting for example, but if the employer feels that this

particular student can't make small talk ... football scores on the weekend ... and help put customers at ease, then I think it's not so much the language that's the problem, but the perception of cultural fit that might sometimes get in the way.

Domestic graduate, Commerce

ELP and the ability to communicate socially with colleagues in the workplace was also considered to be important for performing well in the workplace and for job satisfaction.

Like for the job itself, I guess because it's not just doing the job with the computer, it's also about like talking to the employees and other co-workers. So communication is very important. Besides, because I did some casual work and I find like communications with the co-workers is also important, like during the lunchtime. So how to speak well, especially like speak, like the slang, you know how to speak the slang, you understand how they talk about the footy, is important.

Chinese student, Commerce

Another commerce graduate also commented on the social aspects of work. Although he had been working in information technology support for over a year, he still felt that he lacked the language skills to interact comfortably with his Australian colleagues. This affected his confidence, his workplace relations and his overall job performance.

I feel not very confident to speak to domestic people especially. I think my workmates, some of them may feel, I am not so friendly and sometimes I feel worried about the relationship between my workmates and this can cause my stress.

Chinese graduate, Commerce

Being able to communicate socially with colleagues was frequently cited by international graduates as being important. They understood that being able to do so involved more than simply having knowledge of the technical or professional language; they understood that it also required a range of skills, including social language skills, in order to fit in.

147

> We need to have more socialising skills, as well, like adopting into the culture. And learning informal languages also is important. Yeah, to fit into the society it's really hard.
>
> Korean graduate, Accounting

In addition to the views of students and graduates, the interviews with higher education staff also revealed their view (gleaned from their experience) that international graduates, when compared with domestic graduates, generally faced greater challenges concerning their ELP and successful employment outcomes. Social language skills were identified as important in getting graduates through the interview process and in working successfully once employed. The following comment from a careers officer represented the view shared by most of the staff interviewed.

> The most common issue we hear mentioned is about the ability of international graduates to explain themselves and be understood, and the ability to listen and understand what is being said to them.

The findings from the Arkoudis et al. study thus highlight the importance of international EAL students finding opportunities to develop their social English language skills during their studies. This raises questions about the role and responsibility of higher education institutions and academic teaching staff in ensuring that EAL students do gain the necessary English skills by the time they graduate.

Awareness of employers' expectations

The findings discussed above highlight a number of important issues. One issue is the lack of awareness among some international students about the kinds of skills and attributes sought after by employers. The findings from interviews with international students and higher education staff indicate that international students place the most emphasis on their academic studies and completing their degrees, and perhaps lack an understanding of the broad range of skills and attributes sought after by Australian employers. The following represents the experiences of many other international students and graduates.

> All my CV was denied by the Australian company ... So I'm not so confident about it because I don't know what the company, the Australian companies, I don't know what they expect or they're expecting.
>
> Chinese student, Accounting

The study showed that previous work experience (or lack thereof) seemed to be an important factor influencing the employment outcomes of international students or graduates, yet most of them did not consider part-time jobs in areas unrelated to their field of study as being important for finding work in their chosen field. This is in contrast to the view of the domestic students or graduates, most of whom considered part-time work and diversity of experiences as being highly valued and sought after by employers. As a result, domestic students and graduates focused on building their résumés with a range of experiences, both related and unrelated to their field of study. Domestic students and graduates referred to employers preferring 'a well-rounded' graduate who had demonstrated a range of skills through participation in part-time work, sporting teams or other higher education programs, such as volunteering or mentoring.

The views of international and domestic students and graduates thus differed considerably on the question of how important or valuable part-time work or extracurricular activities were to workplace readiness and employment outcomes. Whereas all the domestic students or graduates believed that diversity of experience and 'well-roundedness' were highly valued and sought after by employers, the majority of international students and graduates seemed to place most importance on their academic studies and relevant work experience in their field of study. It can be argued that domestic students have a more accurate or realistic view of the kinds of skills and attributes valued by employers. We know, for example, that while Australian employers consider ELP to be very important, they also seek well-rounded employees who not only have sufficient ELP but also have the potential to adapt to the Australian workplace, a process facilitated by cross-cultural ability, personality and prior relevant workplace experience (Hawthorne 2007).

While it may be easy to conclude that ELP was the main factor influencing these international and domestic graduates' different employment outcomes, a closer examination of the findings reveals that the issue is complex and that factors other than ELP also influence employment outcomes. This is evidenced by the fact that the majority of international student graduates who participated in this study failed to reach the interview (or pre-interview screening) stage in the application process, which suggests that they failed solely on the basis of their written curriculum vitae, which most students prepared with intensive support from professional career advisers. It follows, then, that ELP had little, if any, influence on employment outcomes before the interview stage. This raises the important question: What are the types of experiences, skills and attributes that are valued by prospective employers and that can be demonstrated in a CV? In other words, what can international students do to build their CV and enhance their chances of being shortlisted for interview?

The issue of accent and prejudice

A number of students questioned whether 'not being a native English speaker' would affect their employment outcomes. This concern was raised particularly by international graduates who had been involved in a pre-interview screening process over the telephone that had unsuccessful outcomes. They believed that they had been disadvantaged because of their non-native accents. The issue of accent was also raised by several students who had just started looking for graduate positions. Although they believed they had high level ELP and had obtained high IELTS band scores (over 7) on entry to higher education, they expressed concern that employers would favour 'some person whose accent is similar with them'.

> I think my communication skills are fine. They're just as good as any domestic. It's the accent that I have a problem adapting to. It's not that I can't understand them, but there's been situation where they can't understand me. And it's only the accent that's an issue.
>
> Indian student, Information Technology

Other students also felt that having a different accent affected employers' perception of an applicant, and that this could be an obstacle to finding work in their chosen field.

> At the interview you're sort of being interviewed along with the domestics. And it's quite obvious, not in terms of just physical appearance but just the way you carry yourself and of course when you open your mouth I think if you sound a lot different, I don't know how it's sort of being marked ... but sometimes it doesn't look as smooth and slick.
>
> Malaysian student, Medicine

In addition to accent, there was the perception among some of the graduates that employers did not want to hire overseas students. While some recognised that this could be due to perceived lack of experience and poor ELP, others believed it was due to some form of racial prejudice, as reflected in the following quote.

> First we just looking for job and, it's really hard for us, like, the overseas student. We've got not experience, not very good English. And just have the degree, it doesn't mean anything and they really didn't want to hire us. And there's very, very little choice to get interview even.
>
> Chinese graduate, Accounting

Higher education staff also mentioned that English language pronunciation appeared to be a particular obstacle for international students in achieving successful employment outcomes. Ten of the interviewees suggested that the workplace might not be ready for speakers of English as a second language, particularly if they were from Asian countries. There may be, for example, greater acceptance of a French English language speaker than a Chinese English language speaker, because there appears to be greater community tolerance towards European languages compared to the tonal languages of most Asian countries. One person referred to this as 'linguistic prejudice'. While some acknowledged that Asian international graduates could often be understood, they also pointed out that employer attitudes to accent could influence their judgements about the level of international graduates' ELP.

The reasons why some international graduates could not find work in their chosen field, despite labour shortages in those fields, were unclear to international and domestic graduates. Inadequate ELP was not considered to be the main reason as even graduates with strong ELP found it difficult to secure work. One domestic Information Technology graduate, whose higher education course had been dominated by international students, spoke about his friends and peers (all of whom had strong spoken ELP), who had intended to live and work in Australia, but had found it too difficult to find work in their chosen fields.

> Unfortunately, the majority of the students I know have returned home because the only jobs they could find was the part-time casual work in restaurants and taxi driving that they did during university. The higher-level jobs were closed to them, or at least that's what they felt.
>
> Domestic student, Information Technology

While these findings suggest that ELP is not the only factor influencing employment outcomes, overall, the study supports the published research showing that ELP represents a powerful component of work readiness and successful employment outcomes. There was a high level of agreement among the participants in our study that ELP is a crucial factor influencing workplace readiness and employment outcomes for all students, international and domestic, although it was not the only factor. If students had low levels of ELP, it was highly unlikely that they would find work in their chosen field.

A question that emerged from the study is whose responsibility it is to develop students' ELP for workplace readiness. The expectation is that graduates come to the workplace ready with these skills. Where do they learn them? Is there scope within the workplace to develop these skills or should they be happening at the level of the higher education institution? Are graduates responsible for developing their English language proficiency for workplace readiness? If so, how can they do this when there are limited opportunities for international students to gain work experience while they study? These questions are explored in the following section.

Improving the workplace readiness of EAL graduates

The discussion presented above highlights the importance of providing more adequate programs that will focus on ELP and workplace communication skills for EAL students in the course of their studies. It is clear that EAL students need opportunities to develop their social English language skills, which will assist their acculturation into the workforce in English-speaking environments. These opportunities exist within and outside their educational institution through extracurricular activities, pronunciation classes offered through the institutions' language and academic skills units, and casual employment or volunteer work where English is the language of communication. Engaging in these activities will assist EAL students to develop a wide range of communication and interpersonal skills for workplace readiness.

Workplace readiness programs

It is important for international students to gain a better understanding of the broad range of skills and attributes sought after by employers in their field of study. Educational institutions can do more to assist international students in this area by explicitly informing them of ways that they can increase their workplace readiness if they intend to find work in English-speaking environments. One way they can do this is to encourage and assist students to seek casual employment that will assist them to develop not only their oral ELP but, importantly, also their understanding of workplace culture and hence their intercultural communication skills.

Most institutions have programs that aim to assist students with job applications, résumés and developing job interview skills. Within these programs, a few of the stand-alone workshops may be targeted at ELP, but only in terms of raising awareness. Given that ELP is a long-term developmental process, little can be achieved in a few two hour sessions. The more innovative programs that are emerging are semester-long subjects offered within courses that focus on developing international students' communication skills in the workplace. These programs can offer insights into potential program design within institutions to enhance ELP in relation to

workplace readiness. The common characteristics of good practice models are those that
- involve ELP, intercultural awareness and job search skills
- make connections with the relevant field of study
- address particular ELP needs of international students, such as pronunciation
- link ELP development to clinical practice or work placement
- involve careers services and academic language and learning unit in developing the program
- are semester long programs that may be offered as part of a course.

Given that students' time in class is limited, perhaps higher education institutions could also consider ways to assist international students find casual work outside the traditional cultural groups, so that they have more opportunities to interact with locals in the workplace, while at the same time developing workplace skills valued by employers. In addition, there would be numerous benefits for international students if departments or schools created closer links with industry and employer groups so that international students would have opportunities to learn about the workplace culture. Having closer links with employer groups could also lead to increased opportunities for international students to gain work placements and internships specific to their field of study.

Summary

This chapter has discussed ELP at the exit point in the ELP development continuum. In doing this, we have considered the influence of ELP on workplace readiness and employment outcomes of EAL students in English-speaking environments. The research shows that international EAL graduates have poorer employment outcomes than their domestic counterparts and that they face more obstacles in finding full-time employment. All the international graduates in our study – regardless of their field of study – expressed that they had found it difficult to find work in their chosen field; a large proportion reported that they had failed, on numerous occasions, to be shortlisted for an interview.

The employment outcomes for international students are an important policy issue for Australia, as in other English-speaking countries which host international students from non-English speaking backgrounds. Much needs to be done to improve international student graduates' workplace readiness and to increase their prospects for finding work in their field of study. ELP represents a high-stakes issue for graduate job access and for mobility within work. While ELP is a key factor influencing their employment outcomes – particularly if graduates have low levels of ELP – the findings from this study show that ELP is not the only or principal issue. Previous work experience and employers' perceptions of graduates' well roundedness is also considered to be important. The well roundedness sought by employers includes graduates' personal characteristics and attributes, the diversity of their experiences and skills, and their cultural fit into the workplace. There is potential to address this expectation through policies and practices that support integrated approaches for enhancing ELP and workplace readiness in educational institutions, as well as by increasing international students' awareness of the value of the experiences and skills they can develop outside of their studies, such as in the course of casual employment in English-speaking environments.

CHAPTER 9

WHAT DOES IT TAKE TO ENSURE ENGLISH LANGUAGE STANDARDS?

This book has considered how higher education institutions can adopt a developmental model of English language proficiency within their policies and practices to ensure the ELP standards of their graduates. This model requires attention to embedding ELP in the teaching, learning and assessment practice within higher education courses, and an increased focus on ensuring the exit ELP standards of graduating students. Many institutions already have a range of policies and mechanisms to support students in improving their English language skills. These functions are, however, frequently marginal to core institutional activities and peripheral to disciplinary practices. Institutions need to ensure that all students who graduate have the requisite skills, knowledge and capabilities to advance to further study or employment.

Higher education institutions have largely focused their energies on assessing the readiness of students with English as an additional language to study effectively in higher education institutions. Entry standards are important and measuring them is a necessary part of ensuring ELP standards. But it is only part of the picture. Far less attention is being given to understanding exit standards and to ensuring that students graduate with the English language skills required for employment and further study. Some believe that in order to address this, higher education institutions should adopt English language testing upon completion of the degree, but it is unclear whether this alone would solve the problem. Far too much importance has been placed on exit ELP testing as the solution to what is a complex issue. We know very little about the validity and reliability of current language tests to indicate readiness for employability, tests that have been developed for entry to higher education study. We require a stronger evidence-based approach that can inform decisions about the appropriateness of English language exit tests. Even if exit tests were the solution, institutions would still need to embed ELP within learning, teaching and assessment practices to increase the potential for graduating students to achieve required results. What happens if graduates fail to achieve the necessary English language test score for professional employment or further study? Indeed, how would the sector be able to address the possibility that EAL students receive a lower exit score than what is required for entry to the course? These scenarios are possible and risk the quality of higher education around the world. Testing alone will not address the issue of ELP standards in higher education. More sophisticated machinery is needed to assess ELP within disciplinary contexts and to be able to link it to identified learning outcomes.

The first chapter of this book introduced a model that considers three key stages in the journey of an EAL student through their higher education studies. The journey begins with students' readiness to commence study and touches on their general academic and social communicative language ability. It moves on to their higher education experience and their engagement with disciplinary teaching, learning and assessment tasks, which touches on the specific academic and social communicative language ability that is required within their discipline. It concludes with students' exit from study and their readiness to enter a profession or to move on to further study, and considers their professional and social communicative language ability. As the book has progressed, each of these stages has been considered in turn and suggestions for improvements in institution policies and practice have been provided. Now each of these are reviewed, and to conclude, the implications for practice at the institutional, curriculum and individual academic levels are considered.

Entry

Entry standards are, as discussed, a difficult area for institutions to monitor. Many EAL students enter higher education institutions without necessarily gaining entry through an English language test score. They may arrive from an English-medium high school, a vocational training institution, from foundation studies or an institution offering English Language Intensive Courses for Overseas Students (ELICOS). In all such cases, it would be a mistake to assume that such EAL students have sufficiently proficient English to be able to succeed with their studies. Empirical studies that investigate how students who enter higher education institutions via different pathways fare during their studies are limited in number, and those that are available tend to have contradictory results. Nevertheless, it is highly likely that an absence of consistent enrolment policies for all students enables some with inadequate English skills to gain admittance to higher education institutions. Not only does this cause problems for teaching and learning, but it can also be very distressing for students who struggle to cope with studies due to an inability to either comprehend what is expected of them or to respond appropriately. Institutions have a responsibility to ensure that all enrolling students have the academic credentials and the English language skills required to have a good chance of succeeding in their studies. It would thus seem sensible that consistent and rigorous approaches are used in monitoring the English language proficiency of prospective students.

The various measures of ELP recognised for entry purposes only indicate whether students are ready to commence as opposed to successfully complete higher education studies. As has been discussed, the array of tests available to students, including the International English Language Testing System (IELTS), Test of English as a Foreign Language (TOEFL), Certificate in Advanced English (CAE) and Pearson Test of English (PTE), and the absence of scientific equivalency studies to compare them, makes the interpretation of test results extremely difficult. Comparing tests using the Council of Europe's Common European Framework of Reference for Languages can reduce some of the confusion. It is important that those involved in determining and administering English language entrance standards receive training that touches on interpreting test results. Training needs to introduce the variety of components that make up the broad productive skills of speaking and writing and the receptive skills of listening and reading. It should also highlight the different ways in which the main English language tests assess each component. While understanding the complexities of the English language and its assessment is important, it is not an adequate measure of ensuring that all enrolling EAL students have sufficient English to be able to cope with their courses of study. It is also vital to acknowledge disciplinary differences. Because English language skills demanded of students vary considerably from one discipline to another, a nuanced approach to enrolment is required.

While developing a greater understanding of English language tests and applying entry requirement with reference to the varying demands of different disciplines is important, it does not take away the fundamental flaw in a reliance on the assessment of English language proficiency: it does not necessarily correspond with academic performance. There is very little evidence that students who perform well in English language tests also perform well in their academic studies. Indeed, the ability of an individual EAL student to cope with, and succeed in, their studies is determined by a whole host of factors that encompass psychological, environmental and linguistic characteristics, as well as prior experiences. This points to the need for institutional assessments of an EAL student's potential to cope with their studies to be holistic, and to incorporate results from English language tests as well as other evidence, including interviews, references and examples of written work. It may also be worth considering students' academic ability as well as their English language learning history. To do so requires a major change in higher education selection policy and procedures.

Experience

Students' experience during their higher education studies encompasses a number of elements: models of practice, course design considerations, pedagogy and assessment. Some of these can be considered and implemented independent of discipline, but the majority are deeply entwined with disciplinary specificities.

In terms of support strategies, there are a number of possible approaches, from individual student consultations to workshops and formal credit subjects. While each approach has its advantages, the fact that each is external to the curricula that EAL students are following can limit their ability to facilitate English language improvements. Academic language and learning units and centres are commonplace in higher education institutions today, usually serving the higher education community as a whole but in some cases located within specific faculties with large numbers of EAL students. These centres provide support to EAL students in a number of ways, including through the provision of discipline-specific advice on academic skills, English language tuition and advice on academic writing. In addition, an increasing amount of attention is being paid to skills development for academic staff to enable them to enhance learning for EAL students through specific pedagogical strategies, such as small group participation and methods to help develop critical thinking skills.

One of the critical considerations for EAL students to enhance their English language skills is the ability to do so within disciplinary contexts, and there is a growing awareness of the importance of disciplinary-specific support. As the case study presented in Chapter 4 demonstrates, the value of integrating English language and disciplinary learning is great. This approach requires a number of considerations: a thorough needs analysis, support from disciplinary leaders, the availability of relevant English language teaching staff, ongoing collaboration with discipline context specialists and, crucially, appropriate resources.

Reconceptualising the curriculum is another important element for ensuring ELP standards, especially when assessment of ELP within disciplinary learning is concerned. The growing diversity of the student body means that assumptions about the best way to ensure that students gain the skills and knowledge they require within any discipline must take account of the needs of the wide range of students enrolled. This approach requires clarity among academic teaching staff about their roles and responsibilities in developing the English language skills of EAL students. Due to the importance of assessment in sending messages to students about the expectations of them, and hence its influence on students' approaches to learning, particular focus is placed on ways of assessing English proficiency in disciplinary learning. Central to this is the interplay between language and content, between which, inevitably, the lines are blurred. Equally important are the perceptions of academic teaching staff. The empirical data drawn on in this book indicate that there are significant disciplinary differences in the priorities that academic staff place on different components of writing skills and the level of English language proficiency they demand of their students. Many academic staff try to ignore English language factors when they assess student work, which raises the question of whether it is possible to separate ideas from the communication of ideas.

Students should have opportunities to express their disciplinary understandings in spoken as well as written English. The interaction for learning framework provides academics with concrete strategies for enhancing interaction between linguistically and culturally diverse students. It offers opportunities for all students to develop their social communicative language to negotiate cultural difference and find ways that they can effectively engage with each other in their learning and teaching context.

The challenges for institutions and teaching staff in supporting the English language needs of EAL students are magnified when the context is shifted to offshore education. While there are similar concerns in offshore and onshore experiences, more attention is required in offshore teaching to the linguistic and cultural assumptions that underpin the content taught, the teaching and learning approaches adopted and the assessment tasks employed.

Exit

The research on workplace readiness clearly shows that employers place high importance on English language communication skills. High-level English language ability is crucial for positive employment outcomes, and mandatory for entry to many professions, including engineering, teaching, medicine, nursing and accountancy. A common argument is that professionals cannot fully contribute in the knowledge economy if they lack sophisticated spoken and written English skills.

In recent years there has been increased media attention and growing concern about the poor workplace readiness and employment outcomes of EAL graduates. Research with EAL graduates highlights a number of important issues, including the lack of awareness among some EAL students about the kinds of skills and attributes sought after by employers. EAL graduates face numerous challenges in securing employment in their fields of study. Even after they have received professional assistance with preparing their résumés, many do not progress to the next stage in the recruitment process.

Some employers, through concern about ELP standards, telephone graduates to assess their oral ELP. Other graduates who do reach the face to face interview stage confront the challenge of performing in a job interview. Even those EAL graduates who are successful in finding employment in their chosen field report challenges in fitting in at the workplace. This has implications for higher education institutions in providing English language programs that focus not only on students' academic language needs, but that also prepare them for the workplace. To date, programs which take such an integrated approach have been limited.

Higher education institutions have an important role to play in assisting EAL students to develop ELP and workplace communication skills in the course of their studies. Alongside the need for improving academic language skills, EAL students need opportunities to develop their social English language skills, which will assist their acculturation into the workforce in English-speaking environments. These programs should exist within and outside their educational institution through integrated workplace readiness programs, extracurricular activities and casual employment or volunteer work where English is the language of communication. Engaging in these activities will assist EAL students to develop a wide range of communication and interpersonal skills for workplace readiness.

The employment outcomes of EAL graduates are an important policy issue for countries such as Australia where much needs to be done to improve EAL graduates' workplace readiness and enhance their prospects for finding work in their field of study. ELP is a high-stakes issue for graduate job access and mobility within work. There is potential to address this expectation through policies and practices that support integrated approaches for enhancing ELP and workplace readiness in educational institutions, as well as increasing international students' awareness of the value of the experiences and skills they can develop outside of their studies, for example, in the course of casual employment.

What needs to be done?

How can progress be made on the perennial issue of ELP standards in higher education? There is little doubt that current approaches for developing English language during higher education are not adequate. Many academics are overwhelmed by the English language needs of their students and are ill-equipped to deal with them. Most English language support programs are underresourced and operate on the margins of disciplinary teaching and learning. Allegations of soft marking in higher education institutions circulate within the sector and English language challenges do not lie solely with international EAL students. As participation in higher education expands in many countries to include previously underrepresented groups, students' backgrounds and preparedness will be increasingly diverse. All of which points to the need for higher education institutions to get better at developing students' ELP alongside their disciplinary studies. Below three areas that are critical to ensuring ELP standards in higher education are presented.

Institutional commitment

In order to embed ELP development within teaching, learning and assessment practices, leadership is required at all levels. Relevant members of the senior executive, deans and course coordinators are responsible for embedding ELP development. Monitoring and evaluation of ELP development must be included in institutional teaching and learning plans. This may include

- course reviews that take into account students' English language development
- student feedback in subject evaluations
- monitoring and evaluation of student progress during the course of their degree
- feedback from employers
- conducting research that informs higher education policy and practice.

It is also important to adequately resource ELP development. We recommend that a targeted approach to embedding ELP be developed, which means that English language specialists would work closely with disciplinary academics in designing teaching, learning and assessment tasks. If higher education institutions adopt this approach, formalised diagnostic testing across the whole institution would not be necessary. The targeted approach to ELP development would not require that students be identified for ELP development, as this would be incorporated within specific subjects that are identified during course mapping activities (see below).

Develop ELP learning outcomes for the disciplinary context

ELP learning outcomes for graduating students need to be identified for each of the courses offered in a higher education institution. The emphasis of the learning outcomes should be on the English language skills that graduates require in their chosen profession and careers. In terms of guiding and enhancing students' English language development and for measuring students' skills, this is the area in which the higher education sector lacks definitive tools. Only when these have been articulated can ELP be embedded within curriculum design.

Higher education institutions need to do much more to map ELP across degree programs to ensure that language skills are integral rather than peripheral to disciplinary studies and are treated as such by academics and students. We are not suggesting that every subject across the higher education institution be involved in ELP development. This would be too resource intensive. One approach could be to incorporate into teaching and learning strategic plans responsibilities for course mapping. In this way, course coordinators and relevant academics would identify appropriate subjects within a degree that are most appropriate for particular ELP learning outcomes linked to those identified for the degree. These subjects would then become the focus of collaboration between English language specialists and disciplinary academics. Collaboration would not have to be ongoing; once disciplinary academics had developed the skills to integrate ELP into their subject the collaboration could end. Collaboration could also include different models, either within the subject or alongside the subject as adjunct tutorials that are linked to the assessment. Course mapping for English language outcomes will lead to strategic, focused and targeted ELP within identified subjects.

Capstone subjects or experiences integrate graduate capabilities and employability skills, and occur in the final year of a higher education course, usually at undergraduate level. Capstone experiences can provide an alternative to using external tests by utilising integrated ELP and disciplinary assessment at the end of the degree. Capstone experiences and studies provide the culmination of theoretical approaches and applied work practice experiences in the final year of an undergraduate degree. Through assessment of the learning outcomes relevant to the aims of the course they ensure that graduates have developed the knowledge and skills for graduate study or employment. Moderation between academics to ensure reliability of results and benchmarking across institutions can be used to ensure consistency in assessing standards.

Develop robust and trustworthy assessment

Professional development for academic staff will be required to develop English language assessment practices within disciplinary learning. The major challenge here lies in understanding how specialist language assessment can be woven into disciplinary assessment and reporting practices. It is probably best achieved through existing moderation processes in higher education institutions, where academics and English language specialists assess and discuss assessment practices and grading of students' work. Central to developing assessment practices would be criteria summaries that include assessment of disciplinary knowledge and ELP relevant to the discipline. Strategic assessment, which is focused on what matters (making this apparent to students through criteria summaries), will also improve student learning.

In conclusion, if institutions are to get serious about English language standards in higher education, then ELP needs to be considered as developmental. This accommodates the language learning needs of a diverse student population over the course of their educational studies. In an era of massification of higher education, one of the key policy challenges is to create teaching and learning standards that are rigorous but flexible to address the complex needs of students and institutions in delivering quality education.

REFERENCES

Adams, T., Burgess, P., & Phillips, R. (2009). Pathways in international education: An analysis of global pathways enabling students to articulate from secondary school to higher education in a transnational context. *Education Across Borders*, 179–198.

Anderson, V. (2008). *Re-imagining 'Interaction' and 'Integration': Reflection on a university social group for international and local women.* Paper presented at the ISANA International Conference 'Promoting Integration and Education'.

Arkoudis, S. (2006). *Teaching International Students: Strategies to enhance learning.* Melbourne: Centre for the Study of Higher Education.

Arkoudis, S., Hawthorne, L., Baik, C., Hawthorne, G., O'Loughlin, K., Leach, D., & Bexley, E. (2009). *The Impact of English Language Proficiency and Workplace Readiness on the Employment Outcomes of Tertiary International Students.* Canberra: DEEWR.

Arkoudis, S., & Starfield, S. (2007). *In-Course English Language Development and Support.* Canberra: Australian Education International.

Arkoudis, S., & Tran, L. (2010). Writing blah, blah, blah: Academics' approaches and challenges in supporting international students. *International Journal for Teaching and Learning in Higher Education, 22*(2), 169–178.

Arkoudis, S., Yu, X., Baik, C., Borland, H., Chang, S., Lang, I. et al. (2010). *Finding Common Ground: Enhancing interaction between domestic and international students.* Melbourne: ALTC.

Australian Education International. (2007a). *2006 International Student Survey – Report of the consolidated results from four education sectors in Australia.* Retrieved 10 May 2012, from https://www.aei.gov.au/research/Publications/Documents/ISS_2006_CONS.pdf

Australian Education International. (2007b). *Follow-up International Student Survey.* Canberra: Commonwealth of Australia.

Australian Education International. (2007c). Study pathways of international Students in Australia. *Research Paper, 1*, 1–8.

Australian Education International. (2008). AEI international student data YTD August. Retrieved 10 May 2012, from https://www.aei.gov.au/research/International-Student-Data/Pages/InternationalStudentData2008.aspx

References

Australian Education International. (2010). *International Graduate Outcomes and Employer Perceptions*. Canberra: Commonwealth of Australia.

Australian Education International. (2011). Research snapshot transnational education in the higher education sector. Retrieved 10 May 2012, from www.aei.gov.au/research/Research-Snapshots/Pages/default.aspx

Australian Industry Group. (2010). National Workforce Literacy Project. Retrieved 10 May 2012, from www.aigroup.com.au/portal/binary/com.epicentric.contentmanagement.servlet.ContentDeliveryServlet/LIVE_CONTENT/Publications/Reports/2010/8783_Workforce_Literacy_Project_Report.pdf

Australian Universities Quality Agency. (2009). *Good Practice Principles for English Language Proficiency for International Students in Australian Universities*. Canberra: DEEWR.

Australian Universities Quality Agency. (2010). Audits: Universities. Retrieved 10 May 2012, from http://www.teqsa.gov.au/audit-reports.

AVCC. (2005). Australian University offshore quality assurance: Refining not re-defining. Canberra: AVCC.

Bacha, N. N., & Bahous, R. (2008). Contrasting views of business students' writing needs in an EFL environment. *English for Specific Purposes, 27*, 74–93.

Bachman, L. (1990). *Fundamental Considerations in Language Testing*. Oxford: Oxford University Press.

Baik, C. (2010). *Academics assessing linguistically and culturally diverse students in higher education*. Unpublished Doctor of Education dissertation, The University of Melbourne.

Baik, C., & Greig, J. (2009). Improving academic outcomes of undergraduate ESL students: The case for discipline-based academic skills programs. *Higher Education Research and Development, 28*(4), 401–416.

Baird, J. (2009). *When 'Onshore' looks like 'Offshore': Quality assurance with onshore partner providers*. Paper presented at ISANA International Conference, www.proceedings.com.au/isana2009/PDF/paper_Baird.pdf.

Baldwin, G., & James, R. (2010). Access and equity in higher education. In P. Peterson, E. Baker, & B. McGraw (Eds.), *International Encyclopedia of Education* (Vol. 4, pp. 334–340). Oxford: Elsevier.

Barthel, A. (2011). Academic Language and Learning (ALL) Activities. Retrieved 12 December 2011, from www.aall.org.au/sites/default/files/table2-ALLservicesTypesNov2011.pdf

Basturkmen, H., & Lewis, M. (2002). Learner perspectives of success in an EAP writing course. *Assessing Writing, 8*(1), 31–46.

Bayliss, A., & Ingram, D. (2006). *IELTS as a Predictor of Academic Language Performance*. Paper presented at the Australian Education International

References

Conference. Retrieved 23 March 2009 from www.aiec.idp.com/pdf/BaylissIngram%20(Paper)%20Wed%201630%20MR5.pdf

Becher, T., & Trowler, P. R. (2001). *Academic Tribes and Territories: Intellectual enquiry and the cultures of disciplines.* Buckingham: Open University Press.

Benzie, H. J. (2010). Graduating as a 'native speaker': International students and English language proficiency in higher education. *Higher Education Research and Development, 29*(4), 447–459.

Berkenkotter, C., & Huckin, T. (1995). *Genre Knowledge in Disciplinary Communication: Cognition/culture/power.* Mahwah: Lawrence Erlbaum.

Bernstein, B. (1990). *The Structuring of Pedagogic Discourse: Class, codes and control.* London: Routledge.

Biggs, J. (1996). Enhancing learning through constuctive alignment. *Higher Education, 32*(3), 347–364.

Biggs, J. (2003). *Teaching for Quality Learning at University.* Berkshire: Open University Press.

Biggs, J., & Tang, C. (2007). *Teaching for Quality Learning at University.* Maidenhead: Oxford University Press.

Birrell, B. (2006). Implications of low English standards among overseas students at Australian universities. *People and Place, 14*(4), 53–64.

Birrell, B., Hawthorne, L., & Richardson, S. (2006). *Evaluation of the General Skilled Migration Categories.* Canberra: Commonwealth of Australia.

Birrell, B., & Healy, E. (2008). How are skilled migrants doing? *People and Place, 16*(1), 1–19.

Boud, D. (1999). Situating academic development in professional work: Using peer learning. *International Journal for Academic Development, 4*(1), 3–10.

Boud, D. (2001). Introduction: making the move to peer learning. In D. Boud, R. Cohen, & J. Sampson (Eds.), *Peer Learning in Higher Education* (pp. 1–17). London: Kogan Page.

Bretag, T. (2007). The emperor's new clothes: Yes there is a link between English language competence and academic standards. *People and Place, 15*(1), 13–21.

Brown, S., & Glasner, A. (1999). *Assessment Matters in Higher Education: Choosing and using diverse approaches.* Philadelphia: Open University Press.

Bruce, N. (2002). Dovetailing language and content: Teaching balanced argument in legal problem answer writing. *English for Specific Purposes, 21*, 321–345.

Bruce, N. (2008). *'English in the Major' at HKU: A second turn of the academic literacy wheel.* Paper presented at the Language Issues in English-Medium Universities: A global concern.

References

Carroll, J. (2005). Lightening the load: Teaching in English, learning in English. In J. Carroll, & J. Ryan (Eds.), *Teaching International Students* (pp. 35–42). London: Routledge.

Carroll, M., & Woodhouse, D. (2006). *Quality Assurance Issues In Transnational Higher Education – developing theory by reflecting on thematic findings from AUQA audits,* Melbourne: AUQA.

Casanave, C. P., & Hubbard, P. (1992). The writing assignments and writing problems of doctoral students: Faculty perceptions, pedagogical issues, and needed research. *English for Specific Purposes, 11*(1), 33–49.

Castle, R., & Kelly, D. (2004). International education; Quality assurance and standards in offshore teaching: exemplars and problems. *Quality in Higher Education, 10*(1).

Chanock, K. (2007a). Valuing individual consultations as input into other modes of teaching. *Journal of Academic Language and Learning, 1*(1), A131–A145.

Chanock, K. (2007b). What academic language and learning advisers bring to the scholarship of teaching and learning: Problems and possibilities for dialogue with the disciplines. *Higher Education Research and Development, 26*(3), 269–280.

Chapman, A., & Pyvis, D. (2009). Teaching and learning in Australian transnational higher education: Distilling principles of quality from stakeholder accounts. *International Journal of Educational Reform, 17*(3), 208–229.

CNN Money. (2011). And the World's Biggest Companies are ... Retrieved 27 July 2011, from http://money.cnn.com/magazines/fortune/global500/2010/index.html.

Coates, H., & Richardson, S. (2011). *Interim Assessment of Higher Education Learning Outcomes (AHELO) Feasibility Report.* Paris: Organisation for Economic Co-operation and Development (OECD).

Coleman, J. A. (2006). English-medium teaching in European higher education. *Language Teaching, 39,* 1–14.

Coley, M. (1999). The English language entry requirements of Australian universities for students of non-English-speaking background. *Higher Education Research and Development, 18*(1), 7–18.

Connelly, S., Garton, J., & Olsen, A. (2006). Models and types: Guidelines for good practice in transnational education. Observatory on Borderless Higher Education. Retrieved 28 September 2007, from www.obhe.as.uk/products/reports.

Coughlan, S. (2008). Whistleblower warning on degrees: BBC News. 17 June.

References

Council of Europe. (2004). Common European Framework of Reference for Languages: Learning, Teaching, Assessment. Retrieved 28 August 2011, from www.coe.int/t/dg4/linguistic/cadre_en.asp.

Cumming, A., Kantor, R., & Powers, D. E. (2002). Decision-making while rating ESL/EFL writing tasks: A descriptive framework. *The Modern Language Journal, 86*(1), 67–96.

Cushing-Weigle, S., Boldt, H., & Valsecci, M. I. (2003). Effects of task and rater background on the evaluation of ESL student writing: A pilot study. *TESOL Quarterly, 37*(2), 345–354.

Davies, A., Brown, A., Elder, C., Hill, K., Lumley, T., & McNamara, T. (1999). *Dictionary of Language Testing*. Cambridge: Cambridge University Press.

De Vita, G. (2002). Cultural equivalence in the assessment of home and international business management students: A UK exploratory study. *Studies in Higher Education, 27*(2), 221–231.

de Witt, H. (2008). *Changing Trends in the Internationalisation of Higher Education*. Paper presented at the Centre for the Study in Higher Education, University of Melbourne, 6 October 2008.

Department of Education Employment and Workplace Relations. (2009). *Good Practice Principles for English Language Proficiency for International Students in Australian Universities*. Canberra: Commonwealth of Australia.

Department of Education, Employment and Workplace Relations. (2011a). The four elements of the new quality and regulatory arrangements for Australian higher education. Retrieved 27 November 2011, from www.deewr.gov.au/HigherEducation/Policy/teqsa/Pages/Overview.aspx.

Department of Education, Employment and Workplace Relations. (2011b). Tertiary Education Quality and Standards Agency. Retrieved 28 August 2011, from www.deewr.gov.au/HigherEducation/Policy/teqsa/Pages/Overview.aspx.

Department of Education, Science and Training. (2005). *A National Quality Strategy for Australian Transnational Education and Training: A discussion paper*. Canberra: DEST.

Department of Immigration and Citizenship. (2011). Student visa English language requirements. Retrieved 7 August 2011, from www.immi.gov.au/students/english-requirements.htm.

Dobos, K. (2011). 'Serving two masters' – academic's perspectives on working at an offshore campus in Malaysia. *Educational Review, 63*(1), 19–35.

Dressen-Hammouda, D. (2008). From novice to disciplinary expert: Disciplinary identity and genre mastery. *English for Specific Purposes, 27*, 233–252.

Dudley-Evans, T., & St John, M. J. (1998). *Developments in English for Specific Purposes*. Cambridge: Cambridge University Press.

References

Duff, P. (2008). Language socialisation, higher education and work. In P. A. Duff, & N. H. Hornberger (Eds.), *Encyclopedia of Language and Education, Vol. 8: Language Socialisation* (pp. 257–270). New York: Springer.

Dunworth, K. (2008). A task-based analysis of undergraduate assessment: A tool for the EAP practitioner. *TESOL Quarterly, 42*, 315–323.

Dunworth, K. (2009). An investigation into post-entry English language assessment in Australian universities. *Journal of Academic Language and Learning, 3*(1), A1–A13.

Durkin, K., & Main, A. (2002). Discipline-based study skills support for first year undergraduate students. *Active Learning in Higher Education, 3*, 24–39.

Educational Testing Service. (2011a). Compare TOEFL Scores. Retrieved 18 August 2011, from www.ets.org/toefl/institutions/scores/compare.

Educational Testing Service. (2011b). *Make Global Connections to More Qualified Students with the TOEFL Test: A Guide to the TOEFL Test for Institutions.* Princeton: Educational Testing Service.

Elbow, P. (1991). Reflections on academic discourse: How it relates to freshman and colleagues. *College English, 53*(2), 135–155.

Elder, C., & Harding, L. (2011). Language testing and English as an international language: Constraints and contributions. *Australian Review of Applied Linguistics, 31*(3), 34.31–34.11.

Elder, C., & O'Loughlin, K. (2003). Score gains on IELTS after 10–12 weeks of intensive English study. *IELTS Research Reports, 4*, 153–206.

Ellis, R. (1997). *Second Language Acquisition.* Oxford: Oxford University Press.

Farrell, D., & Grant, A. (2005). China's looming talent shortage. *South China Morning Post,* 19 October.

Fegan, S. (2006). International students' expectations of speaking English in Australia. In J. van Rij-Heyligers, S. Carter, & J. Buxton (Eds.), *Intercultural Communications Across University Setting: Myths and realities: Referred proceedings of the 6th communication skills in university education conference* (pp. 13–29). Auckland: Pearson Education.

Ferguson, G. (1997). Cultural differences in academic essay orientations. In Z. Golebiowski, & H. Borland (Eds.), *Academic Communication Across Disciplines and Cultures* (Vol. 2, pp. 32–37). Melbourne: Victoria University of Technology.

Fincher, C., Carter, P., Tombesi, P., Shaw, K., & Martel, A. (2009). Transnational and temporary: Students, community and place-making in central Melbourne. Retrieved 1 June 2010, from www.transnationalandtemporary.com.au/publications/tat_final-report.pdf.

Fiocco, M. (2006). *An Evaluation of a Pathway Program: The students' view.* Paper presented at the Australian Education International Conference.

References

Retrieved 10 May 2008, from www.aiec.idp.com/pdf/Fiocco%20Wed%201630%20MR4.pdf.

Fox, H. (1994). *Listening to the world: Cultural issues in academic writing.* Urbana: National Council of Teachers of English.

Fox, J. (2005). Rethinking second language admission requirements: Problems with language-residency criteria and the need for language assessment and support. *Language Assessment Quarterly, 2*(2), 85–115.

Gallagher, M. (2010). The accountability of quality agenda in higher education. Retrieved 12 December 2010, from www.go8.edu.au/government-a-business/go8-policy-a-analysis/2010/238-the-accountability-for-quality-agenda-in-higher-education,.

Geertz, C. (1983). *Local Knowledge: Further essays in interpretive anthropology.* New York: Basic Books.

Gehringer, E. F., Chinn, D. D., Perez-Quinones, M. A., & Ardis, M. (2005). Using peer review in teaching computing. *SIGCSE, 37*(1), 321–322.

Golder, K., Reeder, K., & Fleming, S. (2009). Determination of appropriate IELTS band score for admission into a program at a Canadian post-secondary polytechnic institution. *IELTS Research Reports, 10,* 69–94.

Graddol, D. (2006). *English Next: Why global English may mean the end of 'English as a Foreign Language'.* London: British Council.

Graduate Careers Australia. (2008). *University and Beyond.* Melbourne: Graduate Careers Australia.

Havnes, A. (2004). Examination and learning: An activity-theoretical analysis of the relationship between assessment and educational practice. *Assessment & Evaluation in Higher Education, 29*(2), 159–176.

Hawthorne, L. (1994). *Labour Market Barriers for Immigrant Engineers in Australia.* Canberra: Australian Government Publishing Service.

Hawthorne, L. (2007). *The Future Impact of Skill Migration Policy Changes on International Student Flows: Rationale for the September 2007+ changes.* Paper presented at The University of Melbourne Forum.

Hawthorne, L. (2009). Demography, migration and demand for international students. In C. Findlay, & W. Tierney (Eds.), *The Asia–Pacific Education Market.* Singapore: World Scientific Press.

Healy, G. (2008). Language test recommended. *The Australian Higher Education Supplement,* 15 October 2008, p. 26.

Holroyd, C. (2000). Are assessors professional? Student assessment and the professionalism of academics. *Active Learning in Higher Education, 1*(1), 28–44.

Hutchings, C. (2006). Reaching students: Lessons from a writing centre. *Higher Education Research and Development, 25,* 247–261.

# References

Hutchinson, T., & Waters, A. (1987). *English for Specific Purposes: A learning centred approach.* Cambridge: Cambridge University Press.

Hyatt, D., & Brooks, G. (2009). Investigating stakeholders' perceptions of IELTS as an entry requirement for higher education in the UK. *IELTS Research Reports, 10*, 17–68.

Hyland, K. (2000). *Disciplinary Discourses.* Harlow: Pearson Education.

Hyland, K. (2002). Specificity revisited: How far should we go? *English for Specific Purposes, 21*, 385–395.

Hyland, K. (2003). Genre-based pedagogies: A social response to process. *Journal of Second Language Writing, 12*(2), 170.

Hyland, K. (2007). Genre pedagogy: Language, literacy and L2 writing instruction. *Journal of Second Language Writing, 16(2)*, 148–164.

Hyland, K. (2009). *Academic Discourse.* London: Continuum.

IEAA. (2008). Good practice in offshore delivery. Retrieved 10 May 2012, from https://www.aei.gov.au/About-AEI/Offshore-Support/Documents/TNE%20Good%20Practice%20Guide%20FINAL.PDF

IELTS. (2007). *IELTS Handbook.* Cambridge: Cambridge ESOL.

IELTS. (2008). Frequency distributions by percentage. Retrieved 10 May 2012, from www.ielts.org/pdf/Guide%20for%20Institutions%20and%20Organisations%202011.pdf

IELTS. (2011a). Guide for educational institutions, governments, professional bodies and commercial organisations. Retrieved 10 May 2012, from www.ielts.org/institutions.aspx

IELTS. (2011b). Institutions – IELTS band scores. Retrieved 10 May 2012, from www.ielts.org/institutions/ielts_scores_explained_dvd.aspx

James, M. (2010). Transfer climate and EAP education: Students' perceptions of challenges to learning transfer. *English for Specific Purposes, 29*(2), 133–147.

James, R. (2010). The academic perspective on academic standards: The challenges in making the implicit explicit. Presentation to AUQA Auditors meeting.

James, R., Krause, K., & Jennings, C. (2010). *The First Year Experience in Australian Universities: Findings from 1994 to 2009.* Melbourne: Centre for the Study of Higher Education.

James, R., McInnis, C., & Devlin, M. (2002). Assessing learning in Australian universities. Retrieved 10 May 2012, from www.cshe.unimelb.edu.au/assessinglearning/index.html

Janopoulos, M. (1992). University faculty tolerance of NS and NNS writing errors: A comparison. *Journal of Second Language Writing, 1*(2), 109–121.

References

Jenkins, S., Jordan, M. K., & Weiland, P. O. (1993). The role of writing in graduate engineering education: A survey of faculty beliefs and practices. *English for Specific Purposes, 12,* 51–67.

Johns, A. (1991). Faculty assessment of ESL student literacy skills: Implications for writing assessment. In L. Hamp-Lyons (Ed.), *Assessing Second Language Writing in Academic Contexts* (pp. 167–180). Norwood, NJ: Ablex Publishing Corporation.

Jones, J., Bonanno, H., & Scouller, K. (2001). Staff and student roles in central and faculty-based learning-support: Changing partnerships. In B. James, A. Percy, J. Skillen, & N. Trivett (Eds.), *Changing Identities: Proceedings of the Australian Language and Academic Skills Conference.* Woolongong. Retrieved 10 May 2012, from http://learning.uow.edu.au/LAS2001/selected/jones_1.pdf

Jordan, R. R. (1997). *English for Academic Purposes.* Cambridge: Cambridge University Press.

Joughin, G. (Ed.). (2008). *Assessment, Learning and Judgement in Higher Education.* Dordrecht and London: Springer.

Kasper, L. (1997). The impact of content-based instructional programs on the academic progress of ESL students. *English for Specific Purposes, 16(4),* 309–320.

Kennelly, R., Maldoni, A., & Davis, D. (2010). A case study: Do discipline-based programs improve student learning outcomes? *International Journal of Educational Integrity, 6*(1), 61–73.

King, A. (2002). Structuring peer interaction to promote high-level cognitive processing. *Theory into Practice, 41*(1), 33–39.

Kingston, E., & Forland, H. (2008). Bridging the gap in expectations between international students and academic staff. *Journal of Studies in International Education, 12*(2), 204–221.

Koehne, N. (2005). (Re)construction: ways international students talk about their identity. *Australian Journal of Education, 49*(1), 104–119.

Lasanowski, V., & Verbik, L. (2007). *International student mobility: Patterns and trends.* Observatory on Borderless Higher Education. September 2007.

Lave, J., & Wenger, E. (1991). *Situated learning: Legitimate peripheral participation.* Cambridge: Cambridge University Press.

Leask, B. (2004). *Transnational Education and Intercultural Learning: Reconstructing the offshore teaching team to enhance internationalisation.* Paper presented at the Australian Universities Quality Forum.

Leask, B. (2009). Using formal and informal curricula to improve interactions between home and international students. *Journal of Studies in International Education, 13*(2), 205–221.

References

Lee, Y., & Greene, J. (2007). The predictive validity of an ESL placement test: A mixed methods approach. *Journal of Mixed Methods Research, 1*(4), 366–389.

Leki, I. (1995). Good writing: I know it when I see it. In D. Belcher, & G. Braine (Eds.), *Academic Writing in A Second Language: Essays on research and pedagogy* (pp. 23–46). Norwood, NJ: Ablex Publishing.

Leki, I. (2007). *Undergraduates In a Second Language: Challenges and complexities of academic literacy development*. Mahwah, NJ: Lawrence Erlbaum.

Long, M. (2005). *Second Language Needs Analysis*. Cambridge: Cambridge University Press.

Lynch, T. (2011). Academic listening in the 21st century: Reviewing a decade of research. *Journal of English for Academic Purposes, 10(2)*, 79–88.

Mackiewicz, J. (2004). The effect of tutor expertise in engineering writing: A linguistic analysis of writing tutors' comments. *IEEE Transactions on Professional Communication, 47*(4), 316–328.

Maclellan, E. (2004). Authenticity in assessment tasks: A heuristic exploration of academics' perceptions. *Higher Education Research and Development, 23*(1), 19–33.

Maley, P. (2008). Skilled migrant visas up by 24 per cent. *The Australian,* 28 July, p. 5.

Marginson, S. (2007). Global position and position taking. *Journal of Studies in International Education, 11*(1), 5–32.

Marginson, S., & McBurnie, G. (2004). Cross-border post-secondary education in the Asia–Pacific region. *Internationalisation and Trade in Higher Education: Opportunities and challenges* (pp. 137–204). Paris: OECD.

Marginson, S., & van der Wende, M. (2009). The new global landscape of nations and institutions. *Higher Education to 2030 Volume 2: Globalisation* (pp. 18–62). Paris: OECD.

McBurnie, G., & Ziguras, C. (2009). Trends and future scenarios in program and institutional mobility across borders. In OECD (Ed.), *Higher Education to 2030 Volume 2: Globalisation*. Paris: OECD.

MCEETYA. (2007). National Protocols for Higher Education Approval Processes. Retrieved 14 March 2008, from www.mceetya.edu.au/mceecdya/national_protocols_for_higher_education_mainpage,15212.html.

Merrifield, G. (2008). An impact study into the use of IELTS as an entry criterion for professional associations – Australia, New Zealand and the USA. *IELTS Research Reports Volume 8*, 283–323.

Moore, T., & Morton, J. (2005). Dimensions of difference: a comparison of university writing and IELTS writing. *Journal of English for Academic Purposes, 4*, 43–66.

References

Morita, N. (2004). Negotiating participation and identity in second language academic communities. *TESOL Quarterly, 38*(4), 573–603.

Murray, N. (2010). Considerations in the post-enrolment assessment of English language proficiency: Reflections from the Australian context. *Language Assessment Quarterly, 7*(4), 343–358.

Neumann, R. (2001). Disciplinary differences and university teaching. *Studies in Higher Education, 26*(2), 135–146.

Newman, M. (2008). Minimum English standard is set too low, tutors say. *Times Higher Education*, 7 February.

North, S. (2005). Different values, different skills? A comparison of essay writing by students from arts and science backgrounds. *Studies in Higher Education, 30*(5), 517–533.

O'Keefe, B. (2006). Articulate workers wanted. *The Australian*, 1 November.

O'Loughlin, K. (2008). The use of IELTS for university selection in Australia: A case study. *IELTS Research Reports Volume 8* (pp. 145–225). Cambridge: Cambridge University Press.

O'Loughlin, K. (2011). The interpretation and use of proficiency test scores in university selection: How valid and ethical are they? *Language Assessment Quarterly, 8*, 146–160.

O'Loughlin, K., & Arkoudis, S. (2009). Investigating IELTS score gains in higher education. *IELTS Research Reports Volume 10*, 95–180.

O'Loughlin, K., & Murray, D. (2007). *Pathways – Preparation and Selection*. Canberra: Australian Education International.

Observatory on Borderless Higher Education. (2007). The growth of English-meduium instruction in East Asia: the key to competitiveness? Retrieved 2 July 2008, from www.obhe.ac.uk/documents/view_details?id=195.

Organisation for Economic Co-operation and Development. (2008). *Education at a Glance 2008*. Paris: OECD.

Organisation for Economic Co-operation and Development. (2010). *Education at a Glance 2010*. Paris: OECD.

Organisation for Economic Co-operation and Development. (2011). *Education at a Glance 2011*: OECD Indicators. Paris: OECD.

Pajares, M. F. (1992). Teachers' beliefs and educational research: Cleaning up a messy construct. *Review of Educational Research, 62*(3), 307–332.

Peach, D. (2003). *Improving the Provision of Learning Assistance Services in Higher Education*. Doctorate of Education. School of Cognition, Language and Special Education, Griffith University, Brisbane.

References

Pearce, J., Mulder, R., & Baik, C. (2009). *Involving Students In Peer Review: Case studies and practical strategies for university teaching.* Melbourne: Centre for the Study of Higher Education.

Pearson. (2011a). Preliminary estimates of concordance between PTE Academic and other measures of English language competencies. Retrieved 7 August 2011, from www.pearsonpte.com/SiteCollectionDocuments/PreliminaryEstimatesofConcordanceUS.pdf.

Pearson. (2011b). Why PTE Academic? Retrieved 14 August 2011, from http://pearsonpte.com/PTEAcademic/Institutions/Pages/home.aspx.

Peelo, M., & Luxon, T. (2007). Designing embedded courses to support international students' cultural and academic adjustment in the UK. *Journal of Further and Higher Education, 31*(1), 65–76.

Phan, L. H. (1999). *Different voices: writers' comparisons of Vietnamese and English academic writing.* Unpublished Masters thesis, Monash University, Melbourne.

Phan, L. H. (2001). How do culturally situated notions of 'polite' forms influence the way Vietnamese postgraduate students write academic English in Australia? *Australian Journal of Education, 45*(3), 296–309.

Phillipson, R. (2006). English, a cuckoo in the European higher education nest of languages. *European Journal of English Studies, 10*(1), 12–32.

Prescott, A., & Hellstén, M. (2005). Hanging together with non-native speakers: The international student transition experience. In P. Ninnes, & M. Hellstén (Eds.), *Internationalizing higher education: Critical explorations of pedagogy and practice* (pp. 75–95). Comparative Education Research Centre, Hong Kong: Springer.

Race, P. (2004). *The Lecturer's Toolkit: A resource for developing learning, teaching and assessment.* London: Routledge Falmer.

Ramsden, P. (2003). *Learning to Teach in Higher Education.* London: Routledge Falmer.

Ransom, L. (2009). Implementing the post-entry English language assessment policy at the University of Melbourne: Rationale, processes, and the outcomes. *Journal of Academic Language and Learning, 3*(2), A13–A25.

Rea-Dickins, P., Kiely, R., & Yu, G. (2007). Student identity, learning and progression: The affective and academic impact of IELTS on 'successful' candidates. *IELTS Research Reports, 7,* 58–134.

Reed, T., Granville, S., Janks, H., Makoe, P., Stein, P., van Zyl, S. et al. (2003). [Un]reliable assessment: A case study. *Perspectives in Education, 21*(1), 15–28.

References

Reid, J. (1992). Negotiating education. In G. Boomer, N. Lester, C. Onore, & J. Cook (Eds.), *Negotiating the Curriculum: Educating for the 21st century*. London and Washington: Falmer Press.

Roberts, F., & Cimasko, T. (2008). Evaluating ESL: Making sense of university professors' responses to second language writing. *Journal of Second Language Writing, 17(2)*, 125–143.

Rovai, A. P. (2002). Sense of community, perceived cognitive learning, and persistence in asynchronous learning networks. *Internet and Higher Education, 5(4)*, 319–332.

Sakyi, A. A. (2000). Validation of holistic scoring for ESL writing assessment: How raters evaluate compositions. In A. J. Kunnan (Ed.), *Fairness and Validation in Language Assessment: Selected papers from the 19th language testing research colloquium*. Cambridge: University of Cambridge Local Examinations.

Sanderson, G., Yeo, S., Thuraisingam, T., Briguglio, C., Mahmud, S., & Singh, P. et al. (2010). Interpretation of comparabilty and equivalence around assessment: Views of academic staff in transnational education. Proceedings of the *Australian Quality* Forum 2010.

Santos, T. (1988). Professors' reactions to the academic writing of nonnative-speaking students. *TESOL Quarterly, 22(1)*, 69–90.

Sawir, E. (2002). Beliefs about language and learning: Indonesian learners' perspectives and some implications for classroom practices. *Australian Journal of Education, 46(3)*, 323–337.

Scarino, A., Crichton, J., & Papademetre, L. (2006). *A Framework for Quality Assurance in the Development and Delivery of Offshore Programs In Languages Other Than English*. The Obervatory on Boarderless Higher Education. Retrieved 3 January 2007, from www.obhe.ac.uk/products/reports/ftpdf/2006-12-01.pdf

Sheehan, M. (2002). *Holistic grading of essays written by native and non-native writers by instructors and independent raters: a comparative study*. Unpublished PhD, University of Rhode Island, Rhode Island.

Skillen, J. (2006). Teaching academic writing from the 'centre' in Australian universities. In D. Ganobcsik-Williams (Ed.), *Teaching Academic Writing in UK Higher Education: Theories, practices and models* (pp. 140–153). Basingstoke: Palgrave Macmillan.

Smith, H., & Haslett, S. (2007). Attitudes of tertiary key decision-makers towards English language tests in Aotearoa New Zealand: Report on the results of a national provider survey. *IELTS Research Reports, 7*, 13–57.

Snow, M. A., & Brinton, D. M. (1988). Content-based language instruction: Investigating the effectiveness of the adjunct model. *TESOL Quarterly, 22(4)*, 553–574.

Song, B. (2006). Content-based ESL Instruction: Long-term effects and outcomes. *English for Specific Purposes, 15*(4), 420–437.

Spack, R. (1988). Initiating ESL students into the academic discourse community: How far should we go? *TESOL Quarterly, 22(4)*, 29–51.

Stefani, L. (2004). Assessment of student learning: promoting a scholarly approach. *Learning and Teaching in Higher Education, 1*(1), 51–66.

Stella, A., & Liston, C. (2008). *Internationalisation of Australian Universities: Learning from cycle 1 audits*. Melbourne: Australian Universities Quality Agency.

Stevenson, M. D., & Kokkinn, B. A. (2009). Evauating one-to-one sessions of academic language and learning. *Journal of Academic Language and Learning, 3*(2), A36–A50.

Stoller, F. (2002, April). *Content-based Instruction: A shell for language teaching or a framework for strategic language and content learning?* Paper presented at the TESOL Convention, Salt Lake City, USA.

Study Abroad. (2011). Full degree programs. Retrieved 1 August 2011, from www.studyabroad.com/programs/full+degree+abroad/default.aspx.

Swales, J. (1990). *Genre Analysis: English in academic and research settings*. Cambridge and New York: Cambridge University Press.

Taillefer, G. F. (2007). The professional language needs of economics graduates: Assessment and perspectives in the French context. *English for Specific Purposes, 26*(2), 135–155.

Tertiary Education Quality and Standards Agency. (2010). Sector update. Retrieved 11 January 2011, from www.deewr.gov.au/HigherEducation/Policy/teqsa/Pages/SectorUpdate.aspx.

Tertiary Education Quality and Standards Agency. (2011). Standards discussion paper. Retrieved 17 June 2011, from www.deewr.gov.au/HigherEducation/Policy/teqsa/Pages/TeachingandLearningStandardsDiscussion.aspx.

Topping, K. (1998). Peer assessment between students in colleges and universities. *Review of Educational Research, 68*(3), 253–264.

Trouson, A. (2010). Student nurses face expulsion due to tighter language controls. *The Australian*, 6 August. Retrieved 8 August 2010, from www.theaustralian.com.au/higher-education/student-nurses-face-expulsion-due-to-tighter-language-controls/story-e6frgcjx-1225901996268.

Trow, M. (2006). Reflections on the transition from elite to mass to universal access: Forms and phases of higher education in modern societies since WWII. In J. J. F. Forest, & P. A. Altbach (Eds.), *International Handbook of Higher Education* (pp. 243–280). Dordrecht: Springer.

References

Tsui, A. (2008). *Internationalization of Higher Education and Linguistic Paradoxes*. Paper presented at the Languages Issues in English-Medium Universities: A Global Concern, Hong Kong University.

Turner, J. (2004). Language as academic purpose. *Journal of English for Academic Purposes, 3(2)*, 95–109.

University of Cambridge ESOL Examinations. (2011a). Cambridge English: Advanced – Exam Overview. Retrieved 21 August 2011, from http://cambridge-english-advanced.cambridgeesol.org/exam-overview-and-results

University of Cambridge ESOL Examinations. (2011b, 21/8/11). Comparing scores on Cambridge English: Advanced CAE and IELTS. Retrieved 10 May 2012, from http://cambridge-english-advanced.cambridgeesol.org/exam-overview/comparing-ielts-band-scores-cambridge-english-advanced-cae

University of Cambridge ESOL Examinations (2012). Test results: Understanding your Cambridge Advanced (CAE) Results. Retrieved 30 May 2012, from http://cambridge-english-advanced.cambridgeesol.org/exam-overview/test-results

Van Nelson, C., Nelson, J. S., & Malone, B. G. (2004). Predicting success of international graduate students in an American university. *College and University Journal, 80(1)*, 19–27.

Vann, R., J., Lorenz, F. O., & Meyer, D. M. (1991). Error gravity: Faculty response to errors in the written discourse of nonnative speakers of English. In L. Hamp-Lyons (Ed.), *Assessing Second Language Writing in Academic Contexts* (pp. 181–195). Norwood, NJ: Ablex Publishing.

Vann, R. J., Meyer, D., & Lorenz, F. O. (1984). Error gravity: A study of faculty opinion of ESL errors. *TESOL Quarterly, 18(3)*, 427–440.

Vaughan, C. (1991). Holistic assessment: What goes on in the rater's mind? In L. Hamp-Lyons (Ed.), *Assessing Second Language Writing in Academic Contexts* (pp. 111–125). Norwood, NJ: Ablex Publishing.

Velautham, L., & Picard, M. (2009). Collaborating equals: Engaging faculties through teaching-led research. *Journal of Academic Language and Learning, 3(2)*, A130–A141.

Wait, I., & Gressel, J. (2009). Relationship between TOEFL Score and Academic Success for International Engineering Students. *Journal of Engineering Education, 98(4)*, 389–398.

Watkins, D. (2007). *What Works? Is western educational research relevant for educational reforms in China?* Paper presented at the Redesigning Pedagogy: Culture, Knowledge and Understanding Conference, Singapore.

References

Watty, K. (2007). Quality in accounting education and low English standards among overseas students: Is there a link? *People and Place, 15*(1), 22–29.

Weigle, S. (2002). *Assessing Writing.* Cambridge: Cambridge University Press.

Welikala, T., & Watkins, C. (2008). *Improving Intercultural Learning Experiences in Higher Education: Responding to cultural scripts for learning.* London: Institute of Education, University of London.

Wenger, E. (1998). *Communities of Practice: Learning, meaning and identity.* Cambridge: Cambridge University Press.

Wenger, E., & Snyder, W. M. (2000). Communities of practice: The organisational frontier. *Harvard Business Review* (January–February), 139–145.

Wette, R. (2011). English proficiency tests and communication skills training for overseas-qualified health professionals in Australia and New Zealand. *Language Assessment Quarterly, 8*(2), 200–210.

Widdowson, H. (1983). *Learning Purpose and Language Use.* Oxford: Oxford University Press.

Widdowson, H. G. (2004). A perspective on English language teaching. In A. P. R. Howatt, & H. G. Widdowson (Eds.), *A History of English Language Teaching* (pp. 353–372). Oxford: Oxford University Press.

Wingate, U. (2006). Doing away with 'study skills'. *Teaching in Higher Education, 11*(4), 457–469.

Wingate, U. (2007). A framework for transition: Supporting 'learning to learn' in higher education. *Higher Education Quarterly, 61*(3), 391–405.

Winter, W. E. (2000). The performance of ESL students in a content-linked psychology course. *Community Review, 18,* 76–82.

Woodhouse, D. (2006). *The Role of Quality Assurance Agencies in Higher Education in the 21st Century.* Melbourne: Australian Universities Quality Agency.

Woodward-Kron, R. (2007). Negotiating meanings and scaffolding learning: Writing support for non-English-speaking background postgraduate students. *Higher Education Research and Development, 26*(3), 253–268.

Zhang, Y., & Mi, Y. (2010). Another look at the language difficulties of international students. *Journal of Studies in International Education, 14*(4), 371–388.

Zhu, W. (2004). Faculty views on the improtance of writing, the nature of academic writing and teaching and responding to writing in the disciplines. *Journal of Second Language Writing, 13*(1), 29–48.

Zuniga, X., Nagda, B. A., Chesler, M., & Cytron-Walker, A. (2007). *Intergroup Dialogue in Higher Education: Meaningful learning about social justice.* San Francisco: Wiley Periodicals.

INDEX

academic entrance standards 17
academic language
  discipline-specific 63–72
  collaboration with disciplinary academics 43–5
  and English language programs 61–3
  and learning activities in Australian universities 40
  status 48–0
academic language and learning (ALL) 37, 39, 40, 42, 43, 46, 60, 142, 154, 159
  status of staff 48–9
academic literacy 14–15, 81, 138
academic performance 71–2
academic practices in responding to students' writing 85, 86
academic standards 10
academic teaching staff
  and critical reflection 108–10
  curriculum design and assessment 84–6
accent and employment outcomes 150–2
Arkoudis, S. 48–9, 52, 73–4, 90–1, 94–5, 133, 134, 142, 144, 148
assessment
  criteria 57–8
  development 165
  diagnostic 68
  to encourage ELP development 90–2
  and higher education institutions 17–18
  language and content 87–8, 159
  and learning 58
  offshore programs 125–6
assessment expectations and student learning 57–9

Assessment of Higher Education Learning Outcomes (AHELO) 11, 12, 116
Association for Academic Language and Learning (AALL) 39
Australian Education International (AEI) 115, 137–8, 140, 141

Bachman, L. 13–15
Baik, C. 80, 84–6, 90, 132
Barthel, A. 39, 44
Becher, T. 63
Birrell, B. 3, 6–7, 137
Brooks, G. 32–3

Cambridge ESOL Examinations 21, 24, 29
Castle, R. 120
Certificate in Advanced English (CAE) 21, 22–3, 24, 27, 29, 33, 36, 158
Chanock, K. 41, 45, 48
Coates, H. 11–12, 116
collaboration (disciplinary academics with English language specialists) 43–5, 75–7, 126, 163–4, 165
Common European Framework of Reference (CEFR) for Languages 25–7
communicative language ability 13–14
course design and structure 68–9
creative writing 106–7
Crichton, J. 121
critical reflection 56–7, 108–10
critical thinking skills and student learning 56–7
cultural fit at work 146–8
curriculum design and assessment 78–92

Index

creating environments 100–2
developing reflexive processes 107–10
engaging with subject knowledge 104–7
to enhance interaction 93–112
fostering communities of learners 110–11
international and domestic students 94–6
learning framework 97–8
offshore ELP 127–9
planning 98–100
role of staff 84–6
supporting 102–4

diagnostic assessment task 68
discussion-based activities 106
discipline-specific approaches 63–72
support of leaders and disciplinary academics 73–4
discipline-specific programs 72, 73
disciplines, integrating English language programs 73–7
Dressen-Hammouda, D. 64
Dudley-Evans, T. 63
Durkin, K. 62

education, elite to mass to universal 46–9
employers and graduates with EAL 132–4, 148–50
employment
aspirations and experiences of students with EAL 142–4
and English language 6
outcomes, accent and prejudice 150–2
outcomes of students with EAL 136–9
outcomes and workplace readiness (Australian study) 141–2
testing ELP for employment purposes 134–6
English for academic purposes (EAP) 51, 68–9, 72, 76, 77
English in professional situations 4–5
English language development 50–1, 61–5, 73–5

in offshore education 113–30
workshops 42–3
English language entry standards 17–36, 157–9
multiple pathways 18–20
overcoming limitations of language tests 33–5
predictive ability of test results 28–30
setting English language requirements 30–3
tests 20–4
understanding test scores 25–8
English language intensive courses for overseas students (ELICOS) 19–20, 158
English language programs
collaboration with disciplinary academics 43–5
development 75
discipline-specific approaches 63–72
elite to mass to universal education 46–9
evaluating effectiveness 49–51
evaluation 70
hierarchy of disciplines within higher education 45–6
individual consultations 41–2
integrating in the disciplines 73–7
models of practice 39–49
practices to enhance students' learning 51–9
specific or generic? 61–3
strategies to enhance development 59
workshops 42–3
English language specialists 37–8, 39, 41
collaboration with disciplinary academics 43–5, 75–7, 126, 163–4, 165
and discipline-specific programs 73–4
and English language proficiency 48, 62, 65, 66, 68–71, 73–7
highly qualified and flexible 74–5
English language standards 156–65

183

Index

developing ELP learning outcomes 164–5
entry 157–9
exit 161–2
experience 159–61
and higher education 12–16
institutional commitment 163–4
quality drives 9–12
what needs to be done? 162–5
English language testing 6, 13–14, 20–4
for employment purposes 134–6
overcoming limitations 33–5
predictive ability of test results 28–30
proficiency tests 35–6
tests 35–6
understanding test scores 25–8
entry standards *see* English language entry standards

feedback 58–9
Fox, J. 20

Geertz, C. 63
Good Practice Principles 10–11, 60
Graddol, D. 4
grammatical competence 13
group projects in management 106
group work resources for students 104

Hawthorne, L. 20
higher education
  and English language 1–2, 5, 6, 17–18, 47, 124–5
  and English language assessment 17–18
  and ELP 47, 48, 50–1, 59–60, 65, 66, 74, 76, 78, 92, 122, 131–2, 156–65
  and English language standards 12–16, 156–7
  hierarchy of disciplines within 45–6
Hutchinson, T. 62
Hyatt, D. 32–3
Hyland, K. 63–4, 65, 88

IDP Education 21, 135

illocutionary competence 14
individual consultations 41–2
institutional commitment to ELP development 163–4
interaction, curriculum design to enhance 93–112
  creating environments 100–2
  developing reflexive processes 107–10
  engaging with subject knowledge 104–7
  fostering communities of learners 110–11
  international and domestic students 94–6
  learning framework 97–8
  planning 98–100
  supporting 102–4
International Education Association of Australia (IEAA) 121
International English Language Testing System (IELTS) 6–8, 18, 21–4, 30–3, 43, 91, 94, 134–6, 150, 158

James, M. 51, 125–6
James, R. 10
job interviews 138, 144–5, 153, 162
job performance 145–6, 147
Jones, J. 39, 43–4

Kelly, D. 120

language ability, levels in 25
language assessment, post-enrolment 50
language competence 13–14
language skills 2–3
language testing 13–14
Lave, J. 64, 118, 119
learners, communities of 110–11
learning and assessment 58
learning outcomes, quality drives 9–12
Leask, B. 124
lectures, making accessible 52–3
Liston, C. 125
Lynch, T. 30

184

Index

Mackiewicz, J. 63
Main, A. 62
Marginson, S. 5, 114–5
model of practice (English language programs) 39–49
   collaboration with disciplinary academics 43–5
   elite to mass to universal education 46–9
   hierarchy of disciplines within higher education 45–6
   individual consultations 41–2
   status of academic language and learning staff 48–9
   workshops 42–3
Moore, T. 30
Morton, J. 30
multinational corporations 4

needs analysis 66–7, 73
Neumann, R. 63
North, S. 64

Occupational English Test (OET) 134
offshore education, English language development 113–30
   assessment 125–6
   Australian context 115–18
   communities of practice 118–20
   continuities and discontinuities of practice 120–6
   ELP curriculum design 127–9
   role of language in content teaching 123–6
   teaching and learning approaches 124–5
O'Loughlin, K. 12, 19, 28, 42, 73–4, 90, 94, 135–6
online collaborative tools 110–11
Organisation for Economic Cooperation and Development (OECD) 5, 11, 115–6

Papademetre, L. 121
Pearson Test of English Academic (PTE Academic) 22, 24, 29, 30, 158

peer(s)
   review in creative writing 106–7
   and self-assessment tasks 109–10
peer-learning activities 101–2
peer-learning workshops 103
peer mentoring programs 111
plagiarism 55–7
practical strategies to enhance student learning 51–9
   educative approach to plagiarism 55–7
   explaining assessment expectations 57–9
   making lectures accessible 52–3
   opportunities for small group participation 53–5
predictive ability of English test results 28–30
prejudice and employment outcomes 150–2
problem-solving in engineering 99
professional communication 14, 132
professional situations 4–5
Programme for International Student Assessment (PISA) 11
project-based learning 99

reflective writing tasks 109
reflexive processes 107–10
Reid, J. 45
Richardson, S. 11–12, 116

Scarino, A. 121
Scholastic Aptitude Test (SAT) 21
self-assessment tasks 109–10
small group participation 53–5
social interaction at work 146–8
sociolinguistic competence 14
St John, M. 63
Starfield, S. 38, 48–9
status of academic language and learning staff 48–9
Stella, A. 125
Stoller, F. 65
students
   creating environments for interaction 100–2
   fostering interactions between international and domestic 94–6

Index

group work resources 104
interaction for learning framework 97–8
and interactive activities 101
planning interaction 98–100
and regular social groups 102
supporting interaction 102–4
student learning, practices 51–9
assessment expectations 57–9
critical thinking skills 56–7
educative approach to plagiarism 55–7
making lectures accessible 52–3
opportunities for small group participation 53–5
student peer review *see* peer(s); peer mentoring
student perceptions 70–1
subject knowledge, engaging in 104–7

team-based learning 99, 107
Tertiary Education Quality and Standards Agency (TEQSA) 9
Test of English as a Foreign Language (TOEFL) 18, 19, 21–2, 23, 24, 27, 28, 33, 36, 134, 135, 158
testing 6, 13–14, 20–4
  overcoming limitations 33–5
  predictive ability of English test results 28–30
  understanding test scores 25–8
text analysis 67–8
textural competence 14
Trow, M. 46–7
Trowler, P. 63

van der Wende, M. 5

Waters, A. 62
Watty, K. 134, 139
Wenger, E. 64, 118–19
Woodward-Kron, R. 41
work, ELP and finding 144–50
workplace readiness and ELP 131–55
  accent and prejudice 150–2

awareness of employers' expectations 148–50
employers and graduates 132–4
employment aspirations 142–4
employment outcomes 136–9, 141–2
importance of ELP in finding work 144–50
improving readiness of EAL graduates 153–4
social interaction and cultural fit 146–8
testing ELP for employment purposes 134–6
workshops
  ELP 43, 44
  English language development 42–3
peer-learning 103
writing
  academic practices in responding to students' writing 85, 86
  peer review in creative writing 106–7
  reflective writing tasks 109